Books by Nika Hazelton

The Belgian Cookbook

THE
BELGIAN
COOKBOOK

Nika Hazelton

Atheneum

NEW YORK

1970

FOR *Peter de Maerel*

AND *Marie-Louise Stoneham*

About This Book

IN THIS BOOK I've tried to describe Belgian life a little, as I've seen it in Belgium and in the homes of my Belgian friends. It is a very civilized life, as befits a country with a magnificent past of crusader castles, cathedrals and painters and a splendid present as a sophisticated international community. I've also tried to show the background of Belgian cookery, since foreign recipes, without anything about their whys and what-fors, are not very interesting.

The recipes in this book are for dishes that pleased me in Belgium. They do not represent, nor are they meant to represent, the whole gamut of Belgian cookery, or even the greater part of it. There is nothing systematic about these recipes; they are a sampling of personal favorites which my family and my friends have liked, and which I hope may appeal to other Americans. For this reason I have avoided recipes with a mainly ethnic or historical appeal.

I have limited the number of recipes deliberately. Unless a country, such as France or Italy, is so familiar that people want to investigate all the possibilities of its food, I think that too many unfamiliar recipes are apt to dismay. All one wants are some feasible and pleasant dishes, not encyclopedic knowledge.

I have also limited the recipes in this book to Belgian home cooking, dishes that are eaten by families day in, day out. In Belgium, as in all of Europe, home cooking is very different from restaurant cooking. I am speaking of restaurants where one goes to dine rather than restaurants that merely feed. People go to a fancy restaurant to eat things they cannot eat at home, and that they don't expect the home kitchen to produce. Good restaurants have resources that do not exist in a home kitchen. Fish dishes with garnitures of a few mussels, shrimp and oysters are an example of this, such as the ubiquitous *Sole Normande* of restaurant fame, which in Belgium is called *Sole à l'Ostendaise.* How many home cooks, especially in this country, will go out to buy a dozen mussels, three or four shrimp and a few oysters? Maybe for a very special occasion, and even then, just a few, very few people. But in a restaurant, they are there, because many dishes of *Sole Normande* will be cooked.

Another reason why I am against restaurant-type food at home is that almost invariably it has the same depressing do-it-yourself look as a home-sewn dress. This almost-right look, which is a most inelegant look, is even more ruinous than total failure which can be shrugged off. Therefore I feel that home cooks should learn to cook superlative home food that cannot be found in restaurants (as they do in Belgium). If they have any energy left over, they might devote it to useful pursuits such as making money to enable them to eat in fancy restaurants, preferably in Belgium.

Acknowledgments

M Y GRATITUDE goes to all the people in Belgium who gave me so much of their time to make this book possible.

Among them, I wish to thank especially M. Arthur Haulot, Commissionaire Général au Tourisme in Brussels, and Mr. Peter De Maerel, the Director of the Official Belgian Tourist Bureau for the United States in New York. My thanks also to M. Jean Gyory, Chef de Presse, Commissariat Général au Tourisme; M. Jules Baus, Press Officer, SABENA Belgian World Airlines; M. A. Vandendael, Directeur Général de l'Office National des Débouches Agricoles et Horticoles; M. M. Cordiau, of the Association Belge des Brasseries; Mme. Francis Geerts; and Mme. Andre Willième, all of Brussels.

This book could not have been written without the help of Mrs. M. L. Stoneham and Dr. and Mrs. E. Boulpaep, of New York; Mijnheer and Mevrouw R. Goris, Dr. and Mme. C. Troch, and Advokaat and Mevrouw W. Goris, all of Antwerp.

And a hug and kiss to my dear Protectors who showed me so much that I would not have seen otherwise: Mlle. Mimi Henrard and M. Jean-Jacques Baffrey, both of Brussels.

Contents

(xi)

The Belgian Cookbook

I

Introduction

BELGIUM is a small country with a surprising variety of lovely and interesting natural and man-made sights, both ancient and supermodern. The Belgians have charming manners and conservative ways which have not stopped them from living very comfortably with the best modern technology has to offer. What strikes the foreigner at once is the excellent quality of everything in sight, from the tall, perfect garden flowers to the clothing sold in rural open-air markets. And Belgian food, on all levels, is extremely good.

The country is small, slightly larger than Maryland, and heavily populated. There are about 9.5 million people in Belgium, as compared to somewhat more than 3 million in Maryland. The country ranges from the plains that border the North Sea to the Ardennes in the south, which, by Rocky Mountain or even White Mountain standards, consists of hills rather than mountains. The climate is temperate and the weather can be humid or wet and is best ignored. Belgium borders on France, Holland, Germany and Luxembourg. During its complicated and agitated 2,000-year history it has been ruled by the Romans, the Franks, Burgundy, Spain, Austria, France and the Netherlands, all of whom left their mark. It became a nation in 1830 when it demanded to be detached from the Netherlands, and it has been a constitutional monarchy ever since, under the Saxe-Coburg family, who gave Queen Victoria her beloved Albert. The Belgians take their royalty in their stride, without the emotional interest the British and the Scandinavians show for their monarchs. Like the Americans the Belgians are governed by a House of Representatives and a Senate. Though Belgium gets constantly overrun in wars not of its own making, it has the gift of recovery, thanks to the industry of its citizens. Today it is a very prosperous country, and a very civilized one. It is an excellent country for foreigners who want to see and understand a lot in a little time, and have a complete sophisticated change from home.

When Americans think of Belgium, they usually think of Brussels and they also think that all the Belgians speak French. Not so. There are quite a number of other important cities, such as Antwerp, the world's fourth-largest port, historical Bruges, lively Liège, Tournai with its great cathedral, Louvain, the famous university town where Erasmus taught in the sixteenth century, Dinant, Namur, Mons, Ypres, Oudenarde and others, almost all worth visiting. As for the language, there is one definite geographical, cultural and linguistic division in Belgium, that between the Flemish and the Walloons. Both the Flemish and the Walloons have their separate traditions and both have enormously contributed to Europe's civilization by the way of painting, architecture, music and the humanities in general.

The Flemish, more than 5 million of them in the north

of the country, speak Dutch in various dialects. French, also in dialects, is spoken in the southern part by the Walloons. Brussels, in the middle of the country, though located in the Dutch-language area, is bilingual, with more than four fifths of its inhabitants speaking French. Both Flemish and French are official languages. And an insignificant number of Belgians near the German border speak German.

Except in rural districts, English is commonly understood in Belgium, which has become a truly international community. It is the center for military and economic organizations like NATO and SHAPE, the European Economic Community and the Common Market. These have attracted not only tens of thousands of Europeans, but Americans as well. Yet Belgium has kept its own cultural identity. Quite apart from its way of living, an astonishing amount of folklore is alive and well, expressed in highly picturesque, if not downright fantastic carnivals, fairs and religious processions. The Belgians are Roman Catholics, but the Flemish are more religious than the Walloons.

Many Belgians are not religious at all. But they all are extremely hard-working. Belgians are exquisitely polite. Strangers will show you your way, salespeople have the patience of angels, and waiters are friends, even to ladies like myself dining alone in luxury restaurants. And the food is excellent, as we shall see.

II

Belgian Food in General

THE FOOD OF Belgium reflects the differences between the Flemish and the Walloons, and it reflects also the best food of Belgium's neighboring countries. Since this book is about Belgian cooking, I do not think it necessary to go into the French, Dutch and German dishes that are eaten in Belgium, except to say that French cookery predominates and that the *haute cuisine* of the luxury restaurants is French.

What makes Belgian food different is a stress on the quality of the ingredients in a way no longer common in France, and this on all social levels. Belgian cooking does not go in for the thrifty dishes the French concoct so well out of odds and ends, but for first-rate raw materials, preferably home-grown. These are lovingly referred to by place of origin: *Asperges de Malines, Fraises de Wépion, Cerises de St. Truiden, Noix de Bastogne, Porc de Piétron, Jambon d'Ardennes* and *Beurre de Namur* (asparagus from Malines, strawberries from Wépion, cherries from St. Truiden, walnuts from Bastogne, pork from Pietron, ham from the Ardennes and butter from

(6)

Namur) are just a few of the many products which stand for the very best of their kind. Restaurants even advertise their *Cuisine au Beurre* lest they should be suspected of cooking with the lesser spread. I thought the quality of less expensive and convenience foods, such as margarine and cornstarch pudding, store-bought mayonnaise and supermarket cookies, in many cases superior to ours.

In the south of the country, where the Ardennes produces superlative porkers which are made into all sorts of famous hams, bacons and sausages, Walloon cookery uses these savory local delicacies in almost every dish. In the north, the Flemish adore velvety sauces, rich with eggs and cream, for their fish, their fowl and their vegetables; these stamp a dish "*à la Flamande.*" But just as Walloon cookery is in many ways more savory than French cookery, the cooking of Flanders is well seasoned and not at all depressingly bland like that of the Netherlands and northern Germany, with which it has so much in common. A friend of mine who has sailed a great deal on Belgium's numerous canals says that you can't, in the north, always tell by the landscape and language that you are out of Holland, but that you can always tell this by the supermarkets. The Dutch ones are all frozen foods and few seasonings, the Belgian ones a vast array of goodies from *pâtés* to a plethora of fresh herbs like chervil, tarragon, chives, thyme and sage; Belgian cooking is neither garlicky nor heavy on the onion, but it makes an enormous use of shallots, fresh herbs and some spices. Among these, I would consider chervil the national herb and nutmeg the national spice; nutmeg is even used for flavoring ground meat.

What the Walloons and the Flemish have in common is that they both like substantial food, and they love to eat. The fact that there is so much of it and that it is so much richer than American food goes back to a rural tradition and to a cool, damp climate which in the past necessitated a much greater intake of food and fats than you would need in a warm climate. Modern living conditions, especially better heating and less hard physical work, make this no longer necessarily so, but the tradition remains. The climate, though, does make a difference to what one's body can take in. Fats don't agree with me usually, but in Belgium, as in Germany and in Scandinavia, I ate along with the locals and thrived on it. The one thing I have against Belgian cooking, and I am not alone, is the tendency to overcook everything, especially vegetables.

Both the Flemish and the Walloons insist on careful cooking, at home and in restaurants, and they get it. Belgian women really will cook for hours, and their tender loving care does indeed show. I think that today's Belgian home cooking is infinitely superior to what gets produced in most European households. There are many little touches that speak of the Belgian cooks' attention to detail; I am thinking, for instance, of the tiny meat or sausage balls that are lavished on soups or stews and complement their taste and appearance.

The food must also be colorful and well presented. A Flemish friend of mine was once severely reprimanded by her sister-in-law because her stuffed tomatoes had been cut open the wrong way—namely, at the top, at the stem end. This meant that the top slice, used later as a kind of lid on the stuffing, would show the stem end of the vegetable, which was not considered a pretty thing. The proper way to slice the top off a tomato was to do so at the bottom end, the lecture went, turning the tomato upside down, which hides the stem end and shows off the smooth end. The Flemish are particularly fussy about things like this. It isn't really surprising in a people who produced the greatest still-life artists, the sixteenth- and seventeenth-century Flemish painters who heaped their canvases so handsomely with all the good things they loved to eat, the birds, the game, the fish, the lobsters, the vegetables and the fruit, and framed them in flowers.

Flemish or Walloon, and at all social levels, all Belgians have an enormous fondness for their food. They are conservative in their food preferences. Though the number of restaurants in Belgian cities is great, only a few feature foreign food. Nor did exotic dishes from the Congo, the former colony where so many Belgians were born and lived, make an impression on Belgian cooking the way the East Asian *Rijstaffel* influenced the Dutch or curries became part of English cookery. In the families, too, there is little, if any, experimenting with new and unfamiliar dishes, the way there is in America. The Belgian counterpart of a well-to-do American suburban matron would be horrified to serve her guests—or her family, for that matter—an Italian or any other rather foreign or exotic dinner.

Thus, Belgians always eat the same kind of thing, judged on how it is prepared. There is no year of the *quiche*, the *crêpe*, Beef Stroganoff, the *paella*, the Beef Wellington and all the other special dishes which in America come and go like so many other fads. Neither is there the constant talk about dieting among Belgian ladies. Those who do, do it quietly, and with dignity.

There are a number of dishes which all Belgians love passionately and which are found everywhere. To begin with, there are chervil soup and leek-and-potato soup. Alas, fresh chervil, with its incomparable flavor, is almost impossible to come by in the United States. Unless we use it canned and imported, there is no substitute for it, and we have to leave it out of the many dishes that call for this favorite Belgian herb.

As for leek-and-potato soup, it is leek-and-potato soup —very good, but there is nothing new to it. All of Belgium eats much fish and seafood, cooked in a Frenchified manner. A decorative appetizer, typically Belgian, is *Tomates aux Crevettes*, tomatoes stuffed with tiny shrimp bathed in mayonnaise, and *Croquettes aux Crevettes*, deliciously crisp shrimp croquettes which are obviously a specialty of the coast, but which turn up on all menus. So does *Anguille au Vert*, baby eel cooked in a lemony sauce of fresh herbs thickened with egg yolks and usually served cold. And then there are *moules*, mussels, the national mollusk, eaten in the months with an R in them. *Moules*, which are larger and more succulent than French mussels, are most at home in Brussels, where many restaurants do them up in two to three dozen or more lovely ways. To Belgians, mussels are not the appetizer, the introduction to the main course of a meal. They *are* the meal, and foreigners who do not know that you either eat mussels or other things live to regret this when they see the size of the dish filled with mussels that is put before them. Moules are eaten with *frites*, French-fried potatoes. Since these are a national habit of such magnitude, I will deal with them later, together with the *fritures*, the deep-fried foods at which the Belgians excel all other nations.

A Flanders specialty from Ghent that transcends its place of origin is *Waterzooi*; the word is best interpreted as a simmering watery affair. Neither soup nor stew, this delicious compromise is made either with fish or with chicken, which is cooked in a herbed broth later thickened with eggs and cream. *Waterzooi* and its fish or meat are served in a deep soup plate. Boiled potatoes or brown bread and butter go with it, and it makes a marvelous informal meal when it is good—that is, when the sauce is not too thick.

When a Belgian wants to say that he is looking after his own interests, he says he is "defending his *biftek*." *Biftek*, with *frites* and a salad, is Belgium's national dish, the staff of life to young and old, poor and rich. But note the spelling; I am not talking of a beefsteak, a steak in the American sense, which refers to a specific part of a steer's or cow's anatomy. A *biftek*, in Belgium, is an anonymous piece of meat without bone or fat, and it can come from a bovine, calf or pig (never a lamb) or even from a horse. In Belgium, as in France and Italy, horse-meat is better than no meat, and it is not that different from low-quality beef either. A *biftek's* quality and size are determined by the price and the class of the restaurant. Steak, on the other hand, is clearly defined as an *entrecôte*, a rump steak, a *tournedos* and so on, and it also comes with *frites*, as practically everything does. But, nameless or not, the meat arrives at the table with a generous pat of herbed butter.

The Belgian meat dish best known abroad is *Carbonnades Flamandes*, slices of beef and onions slowly stewed for hours in beer and made in as many varieties as there are for goulash. Some people use light beer, some dark, thus changing the flavor, and some thicken the sauce with crustless bread (dark or light) spread with Belgian or Dijon-type mustard, an excellent way of thickening all brown stews. Then there are all the lovely pork products from the Ardennes, which please all of the country. *Jambon d'Ardennes*, smoked ham sliced razor thin, ranks with the great hams of the world, and is on all

Belgian menus. *Boudins* are not puddings, but sausages, which come in many varieties, some of them local. The basic *boudin blanc* is fairly bland; the *boudin noir*, a blood sausage; and all *boudins* are not so very different from their cousins that make the whole of northern Europe happy.

It seems strange to me that the vast forests of America yield so little game when the small forests of overpopulated Europe yield so much. Like all Europeans, the Belgians adore game, and they eat as much of it as they can possibly get, even to importing it from other countries, as in the case of wild boar, *marcassin*, of which there can never be enough. Rabbit, hare, roebuck and, as I said, wild boar are cooked in the various ways of French cookery. So are all the game birds, big and small, wild duck, grouse, snipe, quail, doves, partridge and even thrush. I once had the latter, poor little things, done up deliciously with bacon, juniper berries and *croûtons*, at the Grand Hôtel des Flandres in Namur. Still, I think thrush better in the air, singing. I have not been in Belgium in the fall, during the hunting season, but I am told that anybody with the price of a game license is out there to shoot, with enthusiasm.

The combinations of meat and fruits are among the other dishes that Belgium shares with the cookery of northern Europe. Applesauce and cranberries are the traditional accompaniments for venison and game, prunes an excellent foil for pork. This liking for dried fruits is ancient custom, from the days when these fruits alone broke up the monotony of cabbage and turnip during the long winter.

A Belgian's relationship with his vegetables is different from that of an American. Vegetables are a delicacy, to be appreciated in their own right, rather than the fodder

that gives us our daily vitamins. The tender, pale asparagus from Malines, juicy from ivory stem to pale jade tip
—with what reverence a waiter will announce its presence on the menu! Time and again, people I dined with
asked if the asparagus on the menu was Belgian, and
when told—sometimes without their asking—that it was
imported, they turned it down with the waiter's full
approval. Dipped in a luscious blend of minced hard-
cooked or *au mollet* egg and butter, it really is incomparable eating, the *à la Flamande* sauce being one of the best
for all vegetables that need saucing. Baby carrots, tiny
peas, dazzling white cauliflower, celery, salsifys (oyster
plant) are all marvelous, though I do not share the
Belgian love for their canned state. I have often won-
dered why the Belgians, the Scandinavians, the Germans
and even the French think so very highly of canned
vegetables. Excellent as they may be, they can never
rival fresh ones. Perhaps this comes from their being
more expensive. (This reminds me of those sad Indians
of the American Northwest, described by anthropologist
Ruth Benedict, who ruin themselves entertaining their
guests, on the principle that the more money you lay out
for your entertaining, regardless of the results, the more
honored the guests will feel. "Dear" is not for nothing a
word with a double meaning.) Brussels sprouts, in Brussels, are what they should be—tiny, tender infants rather
than overblown adults. As for the national vegetable,
Belgian endives or *witloof*—that is, "white leaf"—more
about it later, in Chapter 7.

As I said, vegetables do not necessarily accompany a
meat dish in Belgium, nor is a salad an automatic part of a
meal as in the United States. But potatoes are, and
Belgian potatoes are marvelous. Like all the potatoes of
northern Europe, they come in many varieties, and each

variety has a taste of its own, which brings back the obvious truth that among the vegetables of the world, the potato is the most satisfying one.

The sweet tooth of the Belgians, all of them, sticks out like a unicorn's horn. The number of places that sell pastries of every variety is staggering, and not only in the big towns. The reason for this is that in Belgium, as in all of continental Europe, far more cakes are bought than are made at home. No good Belgian, French, Swiss or Italian home cook is expected to be an accomplished pastry chef. This is a reasonable attitude, because no home baker can ever emulate those masters of the *Japonais* and the *Génoise*, the butter cream and the *Fondant*, who have studied their art for years. Thus, when you have guests in continental Europe, the far more elegant —in fact, the only elegant—thing to do is to buy the cakes from a *pâtisserie*, a "good house," as they say in Belgium, all of which have their specialties.

In Belgium, as in Switzerland, there is a distinction among the places that sell cakes. There are the *boulangeries*, the bakers, who make the *bourgeois* pastries that you pick up as you buy your daily bread but would not serve to guests. These include the open-faced pies, such as *Tarte au Riz*, filled with rice pudding, albeit a superior one; *Tarte à la Maquée*, made with a kind of cottage cheese; the *Tarte à la Crème*, custard pie; and the *Tarte au Sucre*, remarkably like Pennsylvania Dutch Shoofly Pie. All the fruit pies, large in size and piled high with apples and plums, cherries and pears, are sisters to the Wähen of southern Germany and Switzerland, more food than dessert. In the bakeries, too, you will usually find the local specialties. I remember a cheese tart in Dinant made with a local cheese whose name I forget, and which, eaten as such, was not a great treat; but

baking transmogrified it into a delicious, creamy filling.
Two other excellent cakes of this homely kind and both
universal favorites are the *Gâteau de Verviers*, a round,
flat yeast coffee cake with a few raisins and a sugary top,
and *La Cramique*, a raisin loaf.

In the *pâtisseries* you will find refined versions of the
various *tartes*, and about all the cakes that French and
Belgian *gourmandise* ever invented, a formidable number. Some have beguiling names, such as *Le Poulet de
Louvain, Le Merveilleux, Le Misérable* and *Le Baiser
de Malmédy*, but these names come nowhere near describing their irresistibly rich and voluptuous nature.
Here, too, the Belgians are conservative in their tastes;
the cakes are always of the same variety. Where they
vary is in the way they are made. In their richness,
Belgian *pâtisseries* are shrines of butter cream, the richer,
the better, and of whipped cream, always sweetened in
Belgium. Belgian *pâtisseries*, like heroes, are known lo-
cally for their excellence, and to be the "first house" of a
town is an accolade similar to four Michelin stars. I have
found it a touching sight to hear distinguished Belgian
industrialists and *haute couture* ladies discuss the merits
of this or that *pâtisserie*. In Brussels it is Wittamer on the
Place du Grand Sablon that makes the heart beat faster.
On Sunday mornings an open-air antique fair is held on
the square, after which you can see the heart-warming
sight of prosperous Belgian gentlemen winding their
way to their Mercedes 600's, sometimes with an antique,
but always with a package from Wittamer.

In a country as attached to its folklore as Belgium, it is
not surprising to find a great many pastries that go back
for centuries. Some of these are national, some local, and
some are sold only on certain occasions. Like so much
historical food, local specialties are frequently variations

on a theme, such as in the spicing, the shaping or the decorating. We are apt to think of these pastries as ginger breads, but many of them do not contain ginger at all, and the French expression *pain d'épices*, spice bread, is the accurate one. You can tell the antiquity of the recipes from the fact that they are sweetened with honey rather than sugar, which was scarce in Europe until the seventeenth century, when the sugar plantations of the Caribbean islands started to export large quantities.

The most beautiful Belgian bakings are the molded spice breads and cookies, from which a cultural history of Belgium could be written. Best known are the *Speculaas*, crisp and rich, which are first pressed in hardwood molds carved by talented sculptors and then baked. These molds, some of which are six feet tall, are now collectors' items. A friend, Peter De Maerel, who is also an art collector with a remarkable collection of Magritte, Delvaux and other great Belgian painters, has an important and interesting collection of old molds; their beauty is beyond my power of description. The *Couques de Dinant*, hard and spicy, are other molded cakes which go back to the Middle Ages. They come in many fantasies, such as the Garden of Eden, pussycats, maidens, hearts, and even snakes, and, like the more ornate Speculaas, they are not to be gobbled down thoughtlessly. In olden days they served as ceremonial and sentimental gifts. What fascinates me especially about these old Belgian bakings is that they show the cultural unity that once was Europe's. Similar spice and ginger breads and similar shapes are to be found not only in the Netherlands, but in Germany and Switzerland. Many of these bakings celebrated St. Nicholas, Belgium's beloved saint of the children. Some are funny, such as the scatological forms

I saw in the Musée de la Vie Walonne in Liège, a treasure house of folklore, which included some tiny spice-bread squares that commemorated the droppings of the Saint's donkey.

Very old too, and baked in magnificently decorative irons, many of which have found their ways into museums, are Belgium's numerous waffles. There are many varieties, made with beer to lighten them, or made with cornstarch from Brussels, or brown-sugar waffles from Liège, waffles to eat fresh and waffles to keep. They do not taste alike by any means, though usually they are eaten hot with butter and sugar or whipped cream.

The Belgians are mad for cookies. Bakery cookies, *pâtisserie* cookies, supermarket cookies, ancient cookies, modern cookies, there are more of them than I can say. The traditional cookies—which include the *Pain d'Amandes*, almond wafers; *Nœuds de Bruxelles*, shaped like pretzels and coated with caramel; macaroons from Baumont; *Kletskoppen* from Bruges, made with nougat —are just a few examples of this sweet bonanza. On the whole, Belgian cookies are on the dry and the crisp side, and they keep well. Once they were made with powdered hartshorn, made from the antlers of the stags and deer which run in the Belgian forests. The modern equivalent for hartshorn is ammonium carbonate (much used in Scandinavia), which gives a lovely, crisp texture to cookies. It can be bought in American drugstores and substituted for equal quantities of baking powder in a cookie recipe.

The grand finale of Belgian sweets is to be found in the candies and the confections. Many of these, such as the nougats and honey balls sold from special stalls at the fairs, are ancient history indeed. And many of the traditional hard candies are local specialties, such as the *Babe-*

lutes of the north and the *Ballons de Tournai*, from the
city with one of Europe's most beautiful cathedrals,
which dates from the twelfth century and has no less
than five great towers.

The Belgians share their love for marzipan with the
other nations of northern Europe. This love goes back
into history; ancient books tell us how ships brought the
precious sugary candy, molded in curious shapes, from
Lübeck to Antwerp in the days of the Hanseatic
League. Marzipan in fancy shapes now turns up around
St. Nicholas Day, December 6, shaped into animals,
fruits and other decorative forms, often too pretty to
wolf down as a candy. But the real pride of Belgium are
the *Pralines*, chocolates of many varieties and of an un-
believable richness and smoothness. I, an old chocolate
hand, think of them as the best I ever ate. They have a
luxurious, made-to-order quality.

Belgian chocolates are bought in surroundings worthy
of them. The *confiseries*, where they are sold, are often
deliciously furbelowed like the *de luxe* containers—
china, crystal, silver, anything that makes a pretty *bibe-
lot*—in which chocolates are put for gifts, costly gifts.
Nor are the chocolates lightly bought; as wine lovers
talk with wine merchants, there are profound discussions
with the *vendeuses* (I dare not use the word salesladies)
with their *haute couture* manner. The choice is painful
at best; I admit Belgians have as strong feelings for their
chocolate makers as Americans have for baseball teams.
In my own circle of friends, the opinions were divided
between the merits of the Maison Neuhaus and the Maison Godiva. I found them both excellent. But the Neuhaus shops in Brussels are pastel *bonbonnières* in themselves and shopping there makes you feel like a
Fragonard. In Belgium, chocolates make the most desira-

ble presents, even for men. The joy with which a box of this fanciest of all candies is received is touching, and almost embarrassing to see, for Americans, who think of a box of candy as that and no more, however good the candy. And in Belgium you don't have to give it in huge quantities; one pound is an elegant gift.

III

Belgian Home Cooking

BELGIAN LIFE revolves around the family to an extent that is astonishing to Americans. One may find this cheering or depressing, depending how one feels about families. An unusual sight to us is the many people in deep mourning for their relatives; in Brussels I saw shops which sell nothing but *deuil*, mourning clothing for women in black and black-and-white. This family feeling, though, gives Belgium an emotional stability that is equally astonishing to Americans. True, the antagonism between the Flemish and the Walloons runs deep at times, but nevertheless the country hangs together. The feeling the Belgians have for their families has enabled them, to my mind, to triumph over the devastations of two world wars and to take in their stride, without losing their national identity, the presence of hundreds of thousands of foreigners who work in Belgium in peacetime.

Belgian home food is family food, substantial and comforting. Breakfast consists of *café au lait*, bread, butter (Belgian butter is always sweet butter), jam and, in the

north, cheese. The usual treats for a late Sunday breakfast are *pistolets*, fresh rolls from the baker, whereas the
weekday bread relies on the trusty round Belgian family
loaf, which does not dry out like French bread. Or it
might be a honey bread, delicious with sweet butter and
cheese, such as I had at a friend's house in Antwerp.

As for coffee, that's what old and young drink. I shall
never forget the smell of coffee which hangs over
Belgian cities at eight in the morning.

The midday dinner is the main meal of the day, for
which the children come home from school and the
husband, on a two-hour break, comes home from his
work. But this is the meal that has changed and is still
changing. The urbanization of life, the traffic jams that
mark a prosperous economy, the employment of women,
and finally the need for a lighter diet are whittling away
at the custom of eating dinner at home in the middle of
the day. However, most Belgians, especially in the country and in the smaller towns, still eat their main meal at
midday, *en famille*. And it is a proper meal indeed, with
a beginning, a middle and an end. The beginning may be
soup, because Belgium is a country of soup eaters, at
noon rather than at night, as in France.

Men especially feel deprived if their dinner does not
start with soup, and I've seen strong men being pitiful
about this. Or there may be an *hors d'œuvre*, such as
fromage blanc, a soft white cheese which is different in
taste and texture from our cottage and cream cheeses,
and which is eaten with spring onions and tiny radishes,
or *Tomates aux Crevettes*, or *Anguilles au Vert*, or *fondue*, fried cheese squares, or a slice of *pâté*, or a bit of
mayonnaise salad—in short, the familiar run of French
family *hors d'œuvres*. *Hors d'œuvres* turn up regularly
on the family table, since Belgians do not like to plunge

right into their main dish the way we do.

Basically, the Belgians like meat, plenty of it, even in their soups, and they spend most of their food money on meat. Belgian workingmen always wonder how the workingmen from Italy, Spain and other countries in the Mediterranean who are part of the Belgian labor force can work hard on rice and pasta. I must add that these foreign workers, once in Belgium, are only too happy to adopt the daily meat habit. Belgian meat dishes are substantial, and they almost always come with either fried or boiled potatoes. As for vegetables and salads, the higher the social level, the more of them, though never as many as in America. All meats and birds are carved in the kitchen and brought to the table on a platter, surrounded by the vegetables. The family dessert may be a cornstarch pudding, a *tarte*, cheese and/or fruit.

In the afternoon the ladies frequently get together in the *pâtisseries* to feast on cakes and gossip. And the children, when they come home from school, get a piece of bread and butter, a banana or some other fruit, or a few simple cookies. At night the supper is a lighter meal, unless it is the main meal of the day. There may be leftovers from lunch, or an egg dish, or cold cuts, cheese and the like.

Sunday is the day for family meals, when parents expect their grown children to come home. Of course, the mobility of our times has changed the family Sunday as so many other things. But the Belgian family Sunday still flourishes. The children don't always like it, but not many have the courage to break with a family custom. Like all Sunday dinners, the Belgian one is more elaborate than a weekday meal. It might begin with Lobster Bisque or fresh asparagus and go on to more fancy fish dishes, such as a *Sole Ostendaise,* or chicken, which in

Belgium is not yet a common meat as in the United States. Or there might be medallions of veal with a rich sauce, or game in season. The dessert could be a *Glace Sibérienne* (that is, Baked Alaska); a *Pudding Diplomatique*, a glorified Bavarian; or an elaborate pastry, such as a *Gâteau St. Honoré* or a *Paris Brest*, from one of the good local *pâtisseries*.

Else the family might go out, *en masse*, for a ride or a long walk, followed by dinner in one of the excellent and often luxurious country or open-air restaurants. I've always been impressed by the many families walking in the lovely Bois de Soignes, Brussels' equivalent of the Fontainebleau, prior to restoring themselves at a gourmet dinner in the various temples of gastronomy of the region, such as the Château de Groenendael. In the good season these expeditions might take a family to the coast, or to the Ardennes, zooming along in their cars. There are just as many gastronomic shrines in those parts, in all parts of Belgium, as in Brussels, and as many people worshipping at their tables.

Such is the importance of Sunday dinner, so I am told, that the hordes of Belgians who fill the country's numerous camping grounds want it to be good, nature or no nature. Just as all scenic spots in Belgium abound in campsites, good restaurants abound near the campsites.

But what never ceased to astound me is that the Belgian young, like their elders, love to eat and that Belgian husbands care passionately about their wives' cooking as if it were the only thing they married their wives for.

Belgian food is a labor of love, which begins with the markets. Open-air markets that go back for centuries and extremely modern supermarkets coexist peacefully in all of the cities. Some of the markets are specialized, such as the Flower Market on the Grand' Place in Brussels, or the Sunday Morning Bird Market of Antwerp, where the farmers bring their chickens in the kind of wicker bird baskets which you see in the old Flemish pictures. I once spent a whole day in the St. Catherine Market in Brussels, where, in the shade of the thirteenth-century Black Tower, the vegetables were unbelievably vivid in color and perfect in shape. I remember the enormous and truly snowy cauliflowers, which looked like so many cumulus clouds; tomatoes of such intense red that it seemed the essence of the color; lettuce and cressonette, the tiny, sharp watercress of Belgium, which were greener than the whole of Ireland. All the vegetables were exquisitely displayed by the vast aproned matrons and sturdy maidens, blond hair high up in beehives. String beans and Belgian endives, by some miracle all of the same length, lay side by side like cigarettes, and so did snowy leeks, while the mushrooms and the potatoes, four different kinds each, had been graded according to size in well-ordered boxes. It was a Flemish picture come to life, including the people.

St. Catherine is also the market place for fish, and for excellent fish restaurants. You can tell what a nation thinks of fish from its fish shops. At St. Catherine, and wherever else I saw them in Belgium, the fish were neatly arranged in separate compartments over sparkling crushed ice, garnished with decorative little parsley bouquets, which set off their lovely, glistening, rosy-white nacreous color that reminded me of rococo interiors. I recognized turbot, sole, flounder, cod, herring, mackerel, salmon, mullet, skate, trout, dourade, lotte, pike, carp, eel, whitefish, lobster, crayfish, tiny and big shrimp, mussels, clams, oysters, scallops, and there were several varieties of fish I did not know.

In spite of open-air markets and small, family-run food stores, Belgians buy most of their food in supermarkets. Some are fancy, others simpler, but in all I was again impressed by the quality of the foods and the variety and elegance of the local and imported *pâtés*, the smoked fish, the mayonnaise salads, the hams and sausages, the truffled *galantines* which have no counterpart in any American gourmet stores, let alone supermarkets. The meats, almost as expensive as ours, were beautiful and presented like jewels. So were the birds: various kinds of chicken—from *poussins* (baby chicks) to *poulets de grain* (grain-fed birds) to plump hens—as well as squabs, ducks, turkeys, already barded for cooking, guinea fowl, game such as quail, snipe, and different cuts of venison and wild boar.

Since much game is now frozen, it is thus available throughout the year. But frozen foods, mercifully, have not yet replaced fresh ones in the popular diet—because of cost rather than aversion, alas. You can buy frozen puff paste, however, which no doubt accounts for the delicious *vol-au-vents*, Beef Wellington, decorative half-moons used for garnishing, and cakes and cookies that you find in Belgian homes, because there are not many home cooks who will make puff pastry and fewer who know how to make it well.

The butter in the supermarkets impressed me too. Basically, there are two kinds, the *beurre de laiterie*, made commercially by the big dairies, and the *beurre de marchand*, made by small farmers, who also pack it by hand and often stamp it with a pretty picture of flowers, cows and other rustic sights. This is the better butter. But there is more to butter. There are butters known by their individuality, and by the place they come from. Belgians with sensitive palates claim they can tell the difference the way wine and tea tasters are able to distinguish their specialties. What I know for sure is that Belgians have strong feelings about butter, feelings prompted by a love that matches Belgian butter consumption.

Belgian holidays mean more delicious food. There is no set Christmas dinner; people serve delicacies too expensive to be enjoyed at other times. A Christmas dinner might start with a rich cream soup or Lobster Mayonnaise. Lobster, in Belgium, is a costly luxury, and Belgians who come to the United States are utterly enchanted with ours, which are so accessible to all. The main dish, in the south, might be *marcassin* (young wild boar) or, in Flanders, *lièvre* (hare). Do not confuse hare with rabbit, though both run and have floppy ears. Hares are wild animals, prized for the delicacy of their flesh. The animals we know as Belgian hares are *lapins*, rabbits, albeit larger than the usual ones, and, like all rabbits, humbler, though no less beloved, meat. The dessert is the *Bûche de Noël*, the chocolaty, cream-filled Yule log of French *pâtisserie* fame. In the spring, Whitsun is a greater gastronomical event than Easter, because there are more fresh things to eat. A spring soup of many fresh vegetables, or new asparagus, could be followed by a veal roast from an animal that never knew any food but mother's milk, surrounded by a variety of fresh vegetables—little carrots and young peas, cauliflowers and pitifully small but superlatively delicious green beans. *Fraises des bois*, wild strawberries, served with thick *crème fraîche*, or a salad of fresh fruits would be the proper festive finale.

The best of wines are drunk on these occasions. Belgium no longer produces any wine as it once did on the Meuse, this being an uneconomic and irrational pursuit;

the Moselle is about as far north as it is possible to grow grapevines. However, a little white wine, called Isca, is produced in the Hoeilaart region. Belgians have finicky wine palates, and you will find the pick of the Clarets and the Burgundies, the Moselles and the Rhine wines, not to mention all the wines from other European countries. What struck me was the excellent quality of the cheap wines that are sold in self-service stores, where the housewives pick them up along with other food while shopping. The other thing that truly amazed me was how much Belgian women know about wine. The national beverage, however, is beer (about which more later in Chapter 8), which very frequently the less sophisticated Belgians prefer to wine.

IV

Belgian Entertaining

BELGIAN SOCIAL LIFE is not casual, and if you are invited for dinner, you may not see the inside of your host's house, but that of a good restaurant. But if you go to somebody's house, it is most likely for a formal dinner. The wife of an important civil servant once told me how she ran her dinners in Brussels. The invitations would be for 7:30. By 7:45 the guests would have arrived and have been served drinks—whiskey for the men, Champagne for the women and tomato juice for those who don't drink. Dinner would be served at 8:15. A bisque of lobster, served plain, without accouterments, would start it. Richly sauced fillets of sole with shrimp and mushrooms, topped with tiny shrimp, could be the fish course. The fish fillets would be folded over three times rather than rolled up because rolled-up fish fillets look insignificant. *Poulet à l'Estragon*, half of a baby chicken cooked with tarragon and served with tiny *rissolé* potatoes, came as the main course, to be followed by a fancifully decorated ice-cream *bombe*. Two rounds of coffee and liqueurs appeared in the salon, but here, too, the ladies abstained. By 11:30 the guests would leave.

Things are different in Flanders. Marnix Gijsen foremost Flemish novelist, celebrated recently his seventieth birthday. He did not want a large party, so only some forty people gathered at Maison Osterrieth in Antwerp, a gorgeous rococo building now inhabited by the Banque de Paris et des Pays Bas. There they feasted on *foie gras*, with old Port; *Homard à la Flamande*, meaning in this case that the lobster swam in a fragrant broth; pheasant in cream sauce served with a potato and *airelles*, the local cranberries; cheese; and an ice-cream creation representing a book with marzipan pages, sugar cover *et al.*, naming the author's books. There were speeches galore and the party did not break up until 1:30 in the morning, having started at 8:00.

The before-dinner cocktail hour, such as we know it, is an alien custom in Belgium, practiced only by people who move in international circles that observe the cocktail hour. The drink you are apt to get in a traditional Belgian home is an *apéritif*. The drinking period is short, which means you must be punctual almost to the minute.

An aspect of guest behavior strange to Americans is the custom of bringing flowers whenever you are invited. Better still, send the flowers beforehand so that the hostess has a chance to arrange them to their best advantage. Flowers play a great role in Belgian social life, and not to send or bring them speaks of very poor manners.

As a guest in somebody's house, you will be rewarded by a dinner to which the hostess has given an enormous amount of thought and care to make it perfect; it is astonishing how often perfection is reached. The dinner will be served beautifully, on fine china and glass, amidst fresh flowers, in a house scrubbed and tidied to make it look its very best. Belgian women, of all social levels, are demon housekeepers. They worship tidy, spotless houses, even if they have to do the work themselves—because it is not easy now to get household help as once upon a time.

They cook like a dream; I've never heard of one who could not, or who did not care about her food. I remember an exquisite dinner in the home of Madame Troch, in Antwerp, when we had Champagne to start with, melon and ham, *Coq au Vin* with potato croquettes, four different cheeses and delicious little fruit tarts. We drank Johannisberg and Nuits St. Georges with this, and Madame Troch, a delicious petite blonde, when complimented upon her wines, said simply: "*Je cure ma cave*," and, indeed, her celler was well looked after. What impressed me as much as the meal was the elegance with which my hostess produced and served the meal all by herself, with an easy smoothness that was extraordinary. I have found this same gift in other Belgian women, and they put American hostesses and their fuss and bother to shame. They are able to do this naturally, without the scores of books which tell American women how to entertain.

Belgian kitchens have the same equipment as ours, though the refrigerators may not be quite as enormous, and freezers and dishwashers not as commonplace yet. But all the smaller things, blenders, electric cookers and the like, are standard equipment.

Belgium is a gourmet's paradise, and you'd think that cookbooks would abound. Far from it. I went into bookstores in every town I visited, and I visited many, to find but a meager number—among which were only three that I would call strictly Belgian. People cook from instinct, from tradition, from reliance on their own gastronomic experiences, adapting recipes to their taste rather than following the written word as we do in America. Yet in our country, where cookbooks multiply like mushrooms in a spring rain, the standard of cooking, both at home and restaurants, is on the decline.

Since Belgian families, on all social levels, are so self-contained, the most important entertaining is done for themselves. Those functions, which may be held in a restaurant or a club, are governed by definite rules. Christenings usually rate only an afternoon coffee or tea for the closest relatives and the godparents, who may be closest relatives. As a christening memento, the family sends out white sugar-coated almonds, or white sugar candies shaped like almonds and filled with chocolate, these latter a cheaper version not approved of by all Belgians. These candies come in charming containers; one which I received lately was wrapped in a miniature lace bonnet. And as I am writing this, I am munching on some gold-wrapped christening candies, inserted among the usual white ones in the shape of a cross. First Communions, and especially engagement parties and weddings get the number-one treatment, with a wide circle of family and friends. Engagements, in Belgium, are only slightly less important than weddings; being taken literally, rather than as the sampling of suitable matrimonial prospects so customary in the United States, they are celebrated with a formal dinner followed by a dance.

A proper wedding, especially in Flanders, is a splendid affair with formal-dress dinner parties for family and friends. There is first the civil wedding, without which a church wedding would not be possible. Belgian wedding dress is formal evening dress, and the sight of fully dressed-up wedding parties emerging from the town hall on their way to church struck me as odd but as rather pretty. When the circle of friends is great, there will be a reception for them after the church ceremony, at home or in a club, where Champagne and little *canapés* and cakes will be served. I remember the exquisite little puff-paste horns filled with a cheese *Béchamel* at a lovely wedding reception in Antwerp, to which I went with a kind friend, Mevrouw Goris. Even more exquisite was the politeness of the party to the totally unknown *amie américaine* who had fallen into their midst; young and old went out of their way to make me feel at home. Then comes the wedding dinner, for the family and the closer friends, where many speeches are made, telegrams read, and many toasts are drunk and where an elephant *pièce montée à la glace* triumphs as the classic wedding dessert. A dance and supper follow, with an elaborate buffet of duck *galantines*, ham from the Ardennes, shrimp and lobster salads, stuffed eggs, invariably a big whole salmon, smoked trout, Russian salad, all most beautiful to look at and to eat.

Of all the things that brought home to me the fact that food is a great labor of love, the menus come first to mind. Not only the restaurant and banquet menus, about which more later, but the wedding menus. These are often magnificent examples of the designer's, the engraver's and the printer's arts, and no money is spared on the paper on which they are produced. Food and wine match, though, interestingly, the dishes are simply named and descriptive, in the deceptive manner of the *haute cuisine*. As a special courtesy, invitations, menus and wedding notices may be printed in Flemish for Flemish-speaking guests and in French for French-speaking guests.

Nicole and Raymond were married in Antwerp, and their menu measures a splendid 28 by 10 inches, illustrated and lettered like an illuminated medieval manuscript. The menu is topped with the couple's names, and there is a text, in Flemish, in which the courses are explained in a very literate, somewhat archaic speech. But the courses are named in French; they were *Homard à la Parisienne, Real Kangarootail Soup, Ris de Veau au Maborange, Le Dindonneau à l'Orange, Glace Sibérienne* and *Moka*. With this the guests drank a Dorpff Traniner, a Grand Cru Pomerol, and Deutz and Geldermann Champagne. I have not the slightest doubts about the quality of the wines.

Three formal dinners, their menu cards reproductions of ancient engravings, celebrated the wedding of Anne and Jan in fashionable Brasschaart, near Antwerp. At one, they dined on *Consommé, Truite Saumonée à la Nantoise, Carré de Veau aux Primeurs, Parfait de Foie Gras de Strasbourg, Glace aux Fraises* and *Moka*, and they drank a 1964 Johannisberg, a 1959 Château Cap de Mourlin, a 1961 Volnai and a 1959 Château d'Yquem. What could be nicer?

For the sake of historical interest, here are two earlier wedding menus, discovered in a museum in Tournai. This was the wedding breakfast of the Prince de Ligne and the Comtesse de Talleyrand-Périgord, in 1851:

DEJEUNER

1   *Hors d'œuvres*
BOUDINS À LA RICHELIEU

Relevés
TURBOT SAUCE HOLLANDAISE
JAMBON FRAIS À LA BORDELAISE

Entrées
VOLAILLES TRUFFÉES
FILETS DE CANETON À LA CHEVALIÈRE
RIS DE VEAU À LA FINANCIÈRE
ASPIC DE FOIE GRAS

IV *(Belgian Entertaining)*

Punch à la Romaine

Légumes
PETITS POIS À LA CRÈME
ASPERGES EN BRANCHES

Rôtis
POULETS DE GRAIN
BÉCASSINES

2 *Froids*
HOMARDS
GALANTINES

Pièces Montées
ROCHER CHINOIS
VIGNE

Desserts
GLACES À LA VANILLE ET AUX FRUITS
ANANAS, FRAISES, ETC.

In 1902 the famille Crombez, at the Château de Taintignie, celebrated in a simpler mood in this manner:

DEJEUNER

Potage Crème Blès Verts
Cassolette Pompadour
Selle de Renne Châtelaine
Croustades Bonloux
Poularde Parisienne
Artichauts Barigoule
Cailles Rôties Compote
Pâté de Colmar
Glace Santiago
Chester Cakes
Ananas, Fruits, Desserts

How to get a husband is a problem in any country, and in Belgium, where matrimony is sacred, it gets to be an even more important problem. To help toward its solution, every year in the middle of May the small, medieval town of Ecaussines holds a *Goûter Matrimonial*, a matrimonial tea party where lads and lasses can look each other over and meet, if they so desire. Strangely enough, it is not an ancient ceremony, dating back only to 1903, when the young ladies of Ecaussines, chagrined that old lovers' customs such as planting the may tree in front of a beloved maiden's house was no longer practiced, and decided to do something about it. Thus, one day, they plastered the town walls announcing that they would give a mammoth tea party on Whitmonday. Hundreds accepted the invitation, and the annual *Goûter Matrimonial* was launched.

I did not have a chance to go to this auspicious event, but a friend of mine, Marcia Willième, went and reported the following: "At least a thousand cars were parked on the outskirts of the town. Thus, one approached by foot, which was good for the atmosphere of it all, as it is a very charming medieval town. There is a gate to the castle farmyard where the event takes place, and as we walked through the farmyard, I noticed a table on a terrace to the side where men and women were sitting, the men on one side, the women on another. It looked like a pre-*goûter*. I thought that perhaps an effort was made to acquaint the participants with each other before the 'public ceremony.' There were many banners, with such inscriptions as: '*Ne pas vivre pour soi seul, voila qui est vraiment vivre*' [Not to live for oneself alone, that is really living] and '*Aimons—la nature est en fleurs*' [Let us love, nature is in full bloom], and the town's people stood by themselves to watch the visitors go by.

"Now, as to how it works. Any interested bachelor may write to the *Directrice* of the *Goûter Matrimonial* and will receive a ticket and a number by mail. He can be of any age or stature—but he should be 'sincerely interested in matrimony.' The girls are all local girls—or women (there were several widows)—and they each receive a number. In front of the town hall, the Master of Ceremonies first reads out a man's number. The man, if he is present, comes forward. Then a girl's number is drawn and read. She comes forward—it seems to be she who comes forward—if she likes the looks of the man. If she doesn't, another girl's number is drawn, and then another if necessary. Some of the poor men eventually sat down again as no woman appeared. It was a bit embarrassing.

"After a couple has been introduced, they must kiss. And after all the bachelors have been raffled off (or forgotten) everybody parades down to the *goûter*.

"The parade was actually quite splendid, with the Mistress of Ceremonies riding in a coach, several floats, and the high-school band and an out-of-town band that marched and did formations in the Grand' Place. People were quite bleary-eyed; the town, I gather, had been drinking steadily for two days previously. In fact, nowhere else in Belgium have I ever smelled whiskey so strongly.

"The *goûter* itself was disappointing except for the speech of the Mistress of Ceremonies. She was buxom and fair-haired in true Rubens style and burst out laughing several times during her speech—all about love with numerous rather graphic physical references.

"The *goûter* area was roped off in the Grand' Place, but it soon appeared that any member of the audience could also sit with the participants upon purchase of a souvenir cup, and the area became overcrowded, with most of the couples having no place to sit. Then some Belgian TV star was introduced, started singing, and I left. But things would continue until late at night, ending with an open-air ball.

"The cake served appeared to be a sort of pound cake and didn't look very interesting or unusual.

"And that was that. It must have been, sixty years ago, rather charming, and it still did have charm, in a way. Actually I have read of several Belgian couples who met each other there."

V

You Eat Well No Matter Where You Eat

Belgian restaurants can be splendid indeed. But
the real revelation about Belgian restaurants is that
they all, no matter how humble, give excellent value for
the money. If they didn't, they wouldn't stay in business
for one day.

To illustrate the point, I would like to describe a
simple meal I had in a café-restaurant in the Marolles, a
popular, lower-income-group quarter of Brussels. It
looked the way all these places look in France or in Belgium—a bar at the rear with a "zinc," two or three
shelves holding all sorts of bottles with colored liqueurs,
punches, and even whiskey and gin. And a set-up for
drawing beer. At one end of the counter stood an *es-
presso* machine surrounded by stands with various cakes
of dubious origin languishing under their plastic covers.
Another stand held numerous plastic potted plants, including flowering ones, with the house cat enthroned
among them. On the dark green, faded walls hung dis-

pirited elderly hand-painted oils of famous Belgian
sights. In the recess behind the two big front windows
stood more plants, this time natural ones, including a
rubber plant and various philodendrons. The tables were
set with white paper cloths, but the napkins were real,
nicely ironed ones; salt, pepper, and two bottles of non-
descript food seasoning stood on the tables. A jukebox
offered a choice of songs, from the Beatles to "April in
Portugal" and Tchaikowsky's piano concerto. The bar-
man-waiter was polishing glasses (I was eating late) and
the motherly waitress was clearing the tables for the
afternoon coffee business. Here I should say that strong
spirits are not sold in Belgian cafés—only beer and *apéritifs*. For hard liquor, you have to go to hotel bars or to
so-called private clubs attached to restaurants. Of course,
there is coffee, which is always good and strong. Specialty coffee stores sell as many as fifteen to twenty
different kinds and blends. Coffee is a Belgian passion,
and from the age of five every Belgian drinks coffee,
though for the younger *aficionados* it is diluted with
milk. The menu, for fifty Belgian francs—that is, one
American dollar—offered soup *du jour* (this day, leek-
and-potato soup) and a choice of gigot of mutton, roast
pork, pork chops, veal loaf, boiled chicken with a white
mushroom sauce, celery-flavored meatballs, rib steak,
filet américain (that is, ground raw beef, which we call
beef tartare), calf's liver, beefsteak, ¼ roast chicken or
veal kidneys. All of these came with a vegetable, such as
creamed endives, or creamed leeks, carrots, or a salad, or
an apple compote. The fish choices were cod with
melted butter and a fillet of dourade with tartar sauce.
This menu could be supplemented with an appetizer of
pâté or mussels tartare or a fish mayonnaise, at less than
50 cents each, and with cheese at 30 or vanilla or choco-

late cream at 15 cents. The meal was properly served with bread. The waitress ladled the soup from a tureen, asking me if I wanted more, and she served me the main course, the well-cooked gigot, from a serving dish. I had started the meal with fish mayonnaise, decorated with tomato and parsley, and did not want any dessert. Thus, for $1.25 I had a meal that in the United States would have cost me at least twice as much.

There are several Belgian equivalents to our drugstore sandwich. Apart from the *frites* stalls (described in Chapter 7), in a tavern you can get two large slices of the marvelous dark bread thickly spread with white cheese and garnished with spring onions and radishes. This, with a glass of beer, might be around a quarter. In the little neighborhood café-bistros you can have soup, *Anguilles au Vert*, snails, pork chops, an omelet, a slice of cod and the inevitable *biftek*, with their *frites*, for anything from 80 cents to $1.50. A glass of beer or one of the excellent Belgian ciders would add 10 cents or so. In Brussels and in the northern cities you can also eat your mussels and oysters in the stand-up bars which advertise their *arrivage journalier*, daily delivery, for less than a dollar.

A country's gastronomical standards are set by the common man, and not by the aristocracy. This is especially true in Belgium, where long before the country became a nation the aristocracy was unimportant compared to the merchants, the artisans and even the peasants. These did lead the good life, as we see in the social history painted by Van Eyck, Memling, Joardaens, Brueghel, Rubens or Snyder, and in the magnificent Gothic town halls and Renaissance guildhouses which, rather than castles, are Belgium's architectural glory. The centuries of foreign rule forced the people to con-

centrate on their private lives in their own private surroundings, rather than cutting sway at court. Thus a city
culture with a basically *bourgeois* society came into
being, if by *bourgeois* we mean a society that prizes hard
work which produces solid domestic comforts. In this
sense, today's Belgium is the *bourgeois* society *par excellence*.

The Belgian common man's love for good food and
his knowledge of it are nowhere better expressed than in
the names of the cobbled narrow streets in the heart of
old Brussels and their restaurants. Behind the miracle of
the Gothic town hall and the gold-edged guildhouses of
the Grand' Place we find the Rue Marché aux Herbes,
where once greens were sold; the Rue des Bouchers, the
butchers' street; the Rue des Harengs and the Rue au
Beurre, the herring and the butter streets, barely wide
enough for one car and one pedestrian on either side.
And among food shops and delicatessen crowding each
other for space here we find some of Brussels' best restaurants (though not the most elegant ones, about which
more later).

Restaurants elbow each other in this paradise of good
and ample eating. The two, chosen at random, which I
think characteristic of this *bourgeois* Belgian eating are
Chez Vincent and the Bon Vieux Temps.

Chez Vincent is a large, popular establishment with a
friendly, rough-and-ready air reminiscent of English
pubs, where $5.00 will buy a gigantic meal and $2.00 a
very adequate one. In the tiled interior, with rough
wooden dining booths and scrubbed tables, under the
smoked Ardennes hams and sausages that hang from the
ceiling, a crowd of what may be called the middle and
lower classes, speaking voluble French or Flemish, had
chosen their dinners from nine *entrées fines*, eight kinds

of *hors d'œuvres variés* and three *hors d'œuvres chauds*, two soups, nine mussels and eleven fish dishes, eight different kinds of eggs and omelets, eighteen *grillades*, broiled meats, three varieties of chicken, six kinds of vegetables and four special sauces, nine choices from the cold buffet, twelve desserts, mostly based on *crêpes*, seven different homemade ice creams and six varied cheeses, plus a dozen or so seasonal dishes and daily specials. The wine list, introduced by a little poem of Baudelaire's, was equally imposing. After a choice of fourteen *apéritifs*, you could get white and red Bordeaux, *rosé*, Swiss Fendant and Moselle by the carafe or the glass, and choose from twelve red Burgundies, including 1966 and 1964 vintages, five white Burgundies, twenty-two red Bordeaux, including 1962, 1964 and 1966 vintages, four white Bordeaux, four wines each from Alsace, the Rhine and the Moselle, five regional wines from Provence, the Rhône and so on, ten different Champagnes, as well as five beers and seven mineral waters. Interestingly, almost all of the wines were also available in the half-bottles which are so rare in the United States. And all of this in a restaurant many of whose customers, in the United States, would not reach much higher than to Howard Johnson for Sunday dinner.

The Bon Vieux Temps, hard to find in a minuscule, very ancient blind alley (though a local baker, whom I asked for directions, accompanied me there in person), is, physically and socially, on a higher level but no less *bourgeois*. Inside, the downstairs bar and the upstairs dining room are furnished with much stained glass, copper and brass and similar antiques, which enjoy a great vogue as restaurant furnishings in antique-mad Belgium. The light was dim in the bar, which helped the portly middle-aged couples to hold hands in what must have

been sinful love, though I find it difficult to associate
middle-aged portly people, especially ladies, with love or
sin. However, it stimulated their appetites, as I was to see
in the small, quiet dining room, where I dined on chervil
soup, fresh trout stuffed with fresh herbs and baked in
papillote (that is, parchment paper) with a little pars-
ley-strewn new potato, and a squab divinely stuffed
with bread crumbs, minced hard-cooked egg, garlic,
fines herbes and juniper berries and cooked in butter in a
charming little copper casserole that came to the table.
For dessert I was fetched by the name of *Dame Blanche*,
which turned out to be vanilla ice cream with fudge
sauce, though of superior quality, and Belgium's most
popular ice-cream concoction. With it I had a lovely
half-bottle of 1959 Pomerol. The whole dinner, with tip,
came to about $7.00.

If I have been talking of Brussels' restaurants so far, it
is because they are typical of the country, and because I
will tell about the eating in the provinces in another
chapter. But in Brussels alone the snooty Michelin guide
stars no less than thirteen restaurants, some of them double (no triple-star ratings are ever awarded outside
France itself). When it comes to describing the *grand
luxe* restaurants of Brussels, it is hard to know where to
begin and what to include. There are so many of them,
all over town and in the suburbs, each with a devoted
and constant following which makes reservations imper-
ative. All of them have impeccable table appointments
and a wealth of fresh flowers. There are *rôtisseries*,
where the meat is grilled over embers of wood; castles
and private mansions transformed into antique-filled
temples of gastronomy; old inns with the sophisticated
rustic *décor* so admired by Belgians; restaurants furnished in the style of the Belle Epoque, plain elegant

restaurants; hotel restaurants and restaurants run by *patrons* whose skill matches their force of character. I am thinking of M. Wynants, of Comme Chez Soi, where the Michelin-starred dishes are *Mousse au Jambon* and *Sole au Riesling*, though more than I admire most food I admired the oysters cooked in Champagne.

Two great restaurants rival each other on the Grand' Place in Brussels. La Couronne is housed in a tall, thin, seventeenth-century building and decorated with Flemish antiques. The other, across the square, is La Maison du Cygne, in an equally splendid and more spacious old guildhouse, where the *décor* is on general Louis XIV lines. The Cygne also sports menu cards which are works of art, and the handsomest I've ever seen in a country where people, even businessmen, consider menu cards delightful souvenirs.

The Cygne became my favorite of all the Brussels *de luxe* restaurants. I never forgot the first meal I had there because I had the pleasure of being surprised by two dishes I had not known before. My *hors d'œuvre* was two petals of rosy Ardennes ham, served with pitifully small and superlatively delicious radishes and hot toast. Then came the plovers' eggs, the first surprise. Two little eggs, prettily speckled in green, lay on a bed of spicy tiny watercress called *cressonette*. The eggs had been half peeled at the top, very correctly so, to reveal a charming color contrast between a nacreous white and the colorful shell. I finished peeling my eggs at the table. The yolk was pale yellow and very delicate in taste, and the herb butter and hot toast went marvelously well with the eggs. It was spring, and no dish could have looked or tasted more like spring. The second surprise was a *Waterzooi* of lobster, a very original specialty served with tiny potato balls. The sauce was creamy, but very light and delicate, proving the difference between the *haute cuisine* of Belgium and the *cuisine bourgeoise*, which likes its cream sauces rather thick and very rich. For my dessert, the waiter stemmed large, perfect strawberries at the table, barely touching them with his hands, and served them with thick *crème fraîche*, the slightly acidulated cream of Belgium and France, which is superior to our heavy cream. The wine was a 1959 St. Emilion. At other times at the Cygne I indulged, without the slightest trace of guilt, in a delicately smoked ham of young boar, a *pâté* of wild doves, a marvelous dish of *Quenelles de Brochet* (pike) with a whiskey sauce, young duck with tiny onions, a pheasant roasted on a spit over an open fire and lamb chops from infant lambs, small infants at that. And I also ate my fill of truffles, baked in their glorious entity, since Belgium is the country of truffles, and this not only in the luxury restaurants. The price of all this *gourmandise?* From one third to half the price of similar establishments in the United States with wines of such distinction that you wonder at their reasonable price.

Apart from the first-class service and the careful cooking, what is it that makes so many Belgian restaurants so outstanding? I think it is the complete freshness of the ingredients. Seafood and vegetables, for instance, are fresh every day, and shopped for every day, and, in the good restaurants, not carried over to the next day. This is as it should be, for when you think of it, no dish can be better than its ingredients.

Now it is time to remark, as the Belgians say, on two ways in which Belgian restaurants differ from ours. The first is that waiters and waitresses are polite and kind to ladies dining alone, guiding their taste with considerable diplomacy in food and wine, and all for the better. In

America no *de luxe* restaurant would admit a lone lady, no matter how respectable, and if it did, it would hide her at a forlorn table and serve her in an equally forlorn manner. I know, because it has happened to me.

The second difference is the Belgian restaurant custom of presenting a guest with a choice of menus at different set prices, which are independent of the *à la carte* menu. These *prix fixe* menus are great bargains. There is nothing derogatory about them since you find them in the toniest of restaurants, where the top menu is apt to be called *Menu Gastronomique*, which, egad, it invariably is. To enlighten my readers, here are four such menus from La Commanderie, a hotel and restaurant housed in a lovely old country manor in Villers-le-Temple, in the Ardennes, which is furnished in that currently fashionable elegant rustic manner. The menus are quite typical, and do not be deceived by the simplicity of the dishes' names; they are by no means simple dishes.

MENU FRS 190 [$3.90]
Pamplemousse glacée au saumon
La bonne soupe du Chef
Brochette à la Hongroise
Coupe Jacques

MENU FRS 320 [$6.50]
Choix de Pâtés

ou

Coquille St-Jacques à la Provençale
La soupe aux cuisses de grenouilles
Tournedos Bordelaise

ou

Côtes d'Agneau Maintenon
Plateau de fromages
Choix de desserts

MENU FRS 2 5 0   [$5.00]
Salade Niçoise
ou
Cocktail de Fruits de mer
La bonne soupe du Chef
Poussin grillé à la diable
ou
Lapereau à la Mère Grande
Choix de desserts

MENU FRS 3 7 0   [$7.10]
Truite amoureuse
ou
Filets de Sole en Farandole
ou
Jambon fumé de marcassin—crudités
La soupe aux cuisses de grenouilles
Cuissot de dindonneau aux morilles
ou
Côte a l'os au poivre vert (2 côtes)
ou
Selle d'Agneau bouquetière
Plateau de fromages
Choix de desserts

VI

Gastronomic Societies

ELGIAN BUSINESS LIFE, which, I'm told, is extremely realistic and visibly profitable, has its tenderer moments when the gentlemen entertain each other at banquets, which they do frequently and in the very best restaurants. Not for them the American banquet circuit of shrimp cocktail, steak and ice cream, but dinners composed with love and style, and style beginning with the handsome menus printed frequently and diplomatically both in French and in Flemish.

The gentlemen belonging to the Association du Brabant des Entrepreneurs Généraux de Tavaux Publics et Privés dined and wined in Brussels on *Le Médaillon de Foie Gras à la Gelée de Pineau, Consommé Madrilène, Escalope de Ris de Veau Grand Duc, Poussin Sauté Cynthia, Petit Soufflé Glace au Grand Marnier*, along with *Sherry Dry Sack, Meursault 1962*, an *Haut Médoc 1959, Roderer Brut* and *Liqueurs*.

It is hard to believe that Belgian restaurant gastronomy could go even further. But it does, in the spreads laid on for the members of Belgium's gourmet societies. There are several, and the one I investigated, on the authority of some *cognoscenti*, was the Club des Gastronomes, presided over by M. F. Geerts. I never did meet M. Geerts, but I did meet his wife, a ravishing brunette, in her house, all fresh flowers, polished antiques and shining silver—in short, *"luxe, ordre et volupté."* The Club takes its trade around, and even abroad, and there is no limit to how far a restaurant *patron* will go for the Club, including printing his menus on linen handkerchiefs and especially designed plates as well as offering lovely raffle prizes. At the Casino in Spa the dear members, who are bankers, lawyers, diplomats, senators, politicians, tycoons or just enthusiastic gastronomes, and their wives, decorated with the Club pin, dined on the following:

Apéritif: Champagne Dom Ruinart
Gewurtztraminer cuvée Comte d'Eguisheim 1964 Beyer
Meursault-Genévrières 1962
Château Chapelle-Madeleine 1962
Château Talbot 1960
Chambole Musigny
Bonne Mares 1961
Château La Tour Blanche 1950 en magnums
Dodine de Canard truffée et pistachée
Petits Homards à la nage sur canapé de légume
Chaud Froid de volaille à l'ancienne
Carré de Charolais à la Dijonnaise
Plateau de Hervé présenté par une délégation de la
Confrérie du Remoudou
Bombe du Casino

And to compensate the members a little for the fatigue of dining, they were given chances of winning either a made-to-order mink coat, an expensive crystal vase or twelve bottles of vintage Champagne.

Even SABENA Belgian World Airlines, the national airline, takes the Club seriously, but then SABENA takes all food seriously. For the Club's Budapest outing the airline produced a menu *tellement soigné*, a Club member told me, that it would have honored any restaurant on the ground. I was not surprised, because the SABENA restaurant at the Brussels airport qualifies as one to which towns people go to dine rather than as a feeding trough for captive travelers, like the restaurants at American airports. Long before I even thought of writing this book, my husband and I had dined impressively at the Aero-Grill on a *Bisque de Homard au Vieil Armagnac, Terrine Maison, Rognons de Veau à la Liégeoise* and *Soufflé Glacé Mandarine Napoléon* which the waiter recommended as samples of Belgian cooking. (I did write it down at the time, because the night before, we had had an atrocious meal at Kennedy's best restaurant.) At another time I went and looked at the SABENA kitchens, where about 2,000 meals a day are cooked from scratch, from fresh ingredients only, which rather impressed me, as did the nearly forty tons of butter needed annually to prepare this airborne *haute cuisine*. But what endeared SABENA most to my husband and myself happened also before I was thinking of this book. A truly horrendous two-hour-long storm delayed the departure of our plane, which sat in the boondocks at Kennedy airport, so that we could not get out. The kind airline, rather than keep us chomping and frothing for our drinks and dinner until we were airborne, gave them to us then and there. I saved the menu on that occasion, since it was a lovely colored lithograph of Liège. This is what made brothers of us orphans in the storm:

DRINKS

Apéritifs

WHISKY SCOTCH OU BOURBON—SHERRY TIO PEPE

MARTINI VERMOUTH—MARTINI DRY—CAMPARI—VODKA

—GIN TONIC

RHUM HIGHBALL—BACCARDI RICKEY—BACCARDI & COLA

—BACCARDI & TONIC

SCREW DRIVER—MANHATTAN—DRY MARTINI

White Wines

CHAMPAGNE MOËT & CHANDON, BRUT IMPÉRIAL OU

HEIDSIECK & CIE, DRY MONOPOLE

MEURSAULT A.C., RESERVE V.S.R.

Liqueurs

SEVE FOURNIER—DRAMBUIE—KIRSCH D'ALSACE JACOBERT

MANDARINE NAPOLÉON—COGNAC—FINE CHAMPAGNE

REMY MARTIN

WHISKY SCOTCH, BOURBON OU CANADIEN

Cold Drinks

BIÈRES BELGES

JUS: ORANGE—PAMPLEMOUSSE—TOMATE—ABRICOT

EAU GAZEUSE—EVIAN—TONIC WATER

COCA-COLA—GINGER-ALE

MENU

FRIVOLITÉS DE COCKTAIL

Hors-d'œuvre

LANGOUSTE À L'ANDALOUSE

JAMBON DE PARME AUX FRUITS

CRÊPE BATELIÈRE

Soups
CRÈME VERA-CRUZ

CONSOMMÉ TREVISE

Entrées
CÔTE À L'OS DES OMBIAUX

POUSSIN AU SAUTERNES

GIGOT DE PRÉ-SALÉ DES GOURMETS

Vegetables
PETITS POIS À LA FRANÇAISE

ARTICHAUTS À LA BARIGOULE

POMMES AMANDINE

POMMES NOISETTE

SALADE GRENOBLOISE

Cheese
LA PIGOUILLE—TOMME GRISE—MERVEILLEUX AFFINÉ

CAMEMBERT—SAINTE-MAURE—BLEU D'AUVERGNE

Desserts
BOMBE GLACÉE CAMARGO

VACHERIN AUX FRAISES

CORBEILLE DE FRUITS

VII

Of Fritures, Frites, Endives and Grapes

THE BELGIANS MAKE the best *fritures* in the world, deep-fried foods that are utterly delicious, crisp, non-greasy and totally addicting. They also eat more *fritures* than anybody else, especially *frites*, French-fried potatoes which should be called Belgian-fried potatoes considering that the Belgians consume them in far greater quantities than the French. What spaghetti is to Italians, *frites* are to Belgians, and Belgian life could no more be conducted without *frites* than American life without peanut butter.

There are indoor *frites* and outdoor *frites* in Belgium, depending on where you eat your French-fries. Indoor *frites* are made instinctively, automatically and to perfection by all Belgian women tall enough to reach the fry pot. Indoor *frites* are not harnessed to just a few dishes, such as fish in England or hamburger in America, but to practically every dish that comes to the table. The only exceptions, as far as I can make out are poached fish and boiled meats, and even then I wouldn't be too sure. But the proficiency of Belgian women with the fry pot does not stop at *frites*. When a housewife wants to give an *allure de fête* to her dinners, she will serve potato croquettes with her meats, though not with fish. From the fry pot also come meat croquettes, shrimp croquettes, the cheese croquettes called *Fondue Bruxelloise* (page 113), which have nothing to do with the liquid Swiss cheese dunk we know as *fondue*, as well as fried fish, crustless fried bread to serve as a bed for spinach and poached eggs, and sandwiches spread with a thick cheese sauce before they are deep-fried. The fry pot also yields little scraped new potatoes or old potatoes cut into balls to look like new ones, both first boiled before being transmogrified into golden nuggets, and excellent deep-fried eggs, to be served with asparagus. Besides, I must not forget the deliciously crisp fried parsley that goes with the *fritures*. And for fried desserts, there is the family of *beignets*, fritters of all kinds, especially apple and pineapple ones. It sounds like an awful lot of fried foods, but then, they aren't all eaten at one time, and they all are irresistible, as I said, making one wish that the noble art of deep-frying had not fallen into such indifference in America.

Outdoor *frites* are eaten in the street. They are made on the street stands on wheels which are found at all strategic locations in all Belgian cities. Or else *frites* are made in the corner of some popular café that advertises *fritures*, where you get your French-fries through a window so that you don't have to go into the café. These *friture* places, where you eat standing up, are the equivalent of our luncheonettes where you can get something simple and quick to eat. All the food is fried to order (though previously prepared for frying) and the oil in the big kettles at the back of a stand or a *friture* is always kept hot so that you don't have to wait as in a restaurant and the prices are much lower.

Outdoor *frites* are eaten by their own sweet selves, dished up in the traditional white paper cone filled to the brim with salted *frites*. If the buyer so wishes, and he always does, a dab of mayonnaise is dropped on top of the potatoes for a few extra pennies. You dip the *frites* into this sauce as you eat them with your fingers, and it beats ketchup all hollow. Though Belgium is the only country I know of where French-fried potatoes and mayonnaise are eaten together, mayonnaise is not the only condiment for *frites*. You can also eat them with tartar sauce or even *Béarnaise*, or with mustard, or pickles or onions soused in vinegar. All of these *frite*-mates are kept in large glass jars on the front shelf of the stand, each jar with a long-handled wooden spoon propped up in it, ready for serving, next to the *cervelas* (a hard sausage) and the hard-cooked eggs which are also standard inventory. Sometimes you can also get other sausages and sweet fritters at the *friture* stands. *Friture* stands are a way of life in Belgium, and it would be impossible to imagine the country without them. They are the nitty-gritty of Belgian eating, where all men become brothers, and where poor men find their dinners.

Once you've eaten French-fries with mayonnaise, they look naked without it, and seem wanting in taste. Mayonnaise, in Belgium, is as much a national institution as the *frites*. In all homes, whatever their social level, it is made fresh, and perfectly. Mayonnaise is used with abandon; as a salad dressing, *vinaigrette*—French dressing—is not nearly as popular as in France.

The *friture* instinct, however, is not an urban phenomenon. You find *fritures* in remote villages, and even in

lonely peasant houses which advertise them written in
soap on the street windows, so that the passing tourist
need not feel deprived.

In the cafés which have large signs saying FRITURES,
you can get other things to eat—short-order dishes like
biftek, fried chicken, pork chops or omelets served with
the ubiquitous *frites*, as well as coffee or beer. I've eaten
in many of these places where for about one dollar you
get a good meal. The really surprising thing, however, is
the quality of the *fritures*, which are crisp and fresh and
dry. This means that the food has been cooked in fresh,
sweet fat which leaves no aftertaste, and at the right
temperature. In the old days all the deep-frying was
done in animal fats, such as beef-kidney fat and lard,
which the experts say give a far better taste than the new
homogenized vegetable fats or cooking oils used today.
But these are easier to handle since they can be heated to
higher temperatures than the former, and thus, not
breaking down as easily, can be used more often before
having to be thrown away. The Belgian ladies worried
about *la diététique* use corn, soybean or peanut oil. But
all the female frymasters I've talked to say that it isn't
the fat, but the skill that matters.

Brussels sprouts and Belgian endives—the words can
be chanted as a rhythmic incantation to their Belgian
motherland. But whereas Brussels sprouts can be grown
—and are grown—anywhere, Belgian endives are grown
only in Belgium. Belgian endives are indeed the national
vegetable, a glamorous one, snow-white stalks tipped in
pale green, crisp to the bite, with a haunting, somewhat
bitter flavor, and, indeed, the most beautiful and appetizing of all winter vegetables.

At various periods of my life, necessity forced me to

grow my own vegetables. I found it such a sobering experience, from planting, weeding and picking the health-giving greens to their canning and freezing, that now I'd just as soon meet a vegetable for the first time on my plate rather than on my knees on mother earth. Thus, when I was invited to go and see how Belgian endives grow, my reaction was apathetic. However, never being one for missing any thrills in a foreign country, be they only vegetable, I did go. And I was glad, because endive growing is such a curious procedure, somewhere between industry and farming, on a small but very profitable scale, and the complete antithesis of the large-scale mechanized farming we are used to in America.

Witloof, in Flemish, or *chicon*, in French, belongs to a variety of chicory, from whose root comes the ersatz coffee used in Europe, especially in France and Italy, to stretch the costly product of the coffee bean. The vegetable was first discovered by chance around the middle of the last century, when some coffee chicory roots that had been lying around in the dark were found to have sprouted some whitish leaves. An enterprising head horticulturist of the Brussels Botanical Gardens, M. Brezier, took up the challenge and grew the first Belgian endives, as we know them, in the cellars of the Botanical Gardens, along with mushrooms. In 1872 the first witloof went to Paris, and from then on it conquered the world.

The two surprising things about Belgian endives are the complicated way in which the vegetable is grown, and the fact that attempts to grow it outside Belgium have utterly failed.

Witloof country lies within a radius of thirty miles or so of Brussels, literally in the shadow of the capital. There the land is very flat, with scattered fruit trees along the straight roads and small farms of one or two or three acres divided from each other by furrows only. The farmhouses are ordinary modern buildings, anything but quaint. What is unusual are the little quonset huts, a few feet high, where the vegetable is grown under corrugated roofs, and the sheds near the farmer's house where it is readied for auction and market. The growing of witloof is a family affair; the whole household pitches in at planting and harvest time. Some 7,000 families make their living from it, calling on the experience handed down from father to son. Yet, however profitable—and witloof growing can be very profitable —this patriarchal way of farming is getting increasingly difficult, for the lack of qualified labor. Young men see easier livings in the factories and in the cities, so that nowadays more and more witloof is grown on industrial lines under big hangars.

There are two distinct processes to witloof farming. The first is the growing of the rootstock, the second the growing of the leaf vegetable. Since the farms are so tiny, growers with large tracts of land in other parts of Belgium sow and raise the chicory in the open air and harvest it just before the frosts set in. The plants are uprooted, the leaves discarded and the endive farmers take home the roots to plant on their farms. This is tight planting indeed; the roots are planted eight, ten or more inches deep in furrows, each root set tightly against the next, and the furrows are extremely close together. Pipes buried some three feet apart in the soil, emanating from a simple central heating system, heat up the soil to temperatures that let the vegetable grow quickly. The witloof season lasts from October through May, and the crops are staggered so that the truly skillful farmer can produce his very early or very late, for the best prices.

The next step, when the roots are securely covered with the rich, soft, crumbly black earth, is to place the little quonset huts over them to shut out light and cold. Furthermore, the huts are lined with straw to protect the delicate plants against sudden changes of temperature. When a crop is needed, the pipes are heated, and the roots sprout leaves. It takes twenty days or so for shoots to pierce the earth above them and to nudge their heads against the straw. Thanks to the black darkness in the huts, the witloof achieves its pure, ghostly color. When the endives measure at least three inches, they are ready for digging. And it is this digging that so impressed me on that windswept day on the plain of Brabant, on a farm that produces about 10,000 pounds of Belgian endives to the acre, an average yield.

The solid Flemish farmer and his two red-faced relatives were down in the field. They had pushed back one of the quonset huts and thrown the protective straw to one side. They were on their knees, digging the crop with four-pronged forks. The crop was an extraordinary and very beautiful sight. Hundreds of firm, snow-white endives, with the faintest pastel yellowish-green topknots, were standing upright in the dark earth, like white birds against an inky sky, resembling sculptures rather than a growing vegetable.

The men heaped the vegetables into baskets and carted them to a shed next to the house, where the farmer's apple-cheeked wife and four other ladies were busy stripping off the soiled leaves and making sure the vegetables were spotless for packing. They graded them for size and thickness, and only the finest stalks went into the boxes lined with tissue paper that we know so well in our American markets. These boxes then went to auction or to the witloof brokers to be sold for their cleaned weight, the perfection of their color, the tightness of their leaves. Loose leaves are money losers, for the stalks have to be retrimmed, a weight loss. Only the firmest, most perfect witloof are exported, a few days from field to American consumers. Their quality is tightly controlled by government regulations, which say exactly how long and how thick an endive has to be to make certain grades.

Even on a large scale, witloof growing means more handwork than other nations are willing to give it. And I've been told that the Belgian endives which at times have been grown in other parts of Europe and even in the United States are not nearly as crisp as the Belgian ones, and inclined to be rubbery. But the popularity of witloof is on the increase, since, among its other virtues, it is so extremely low in calories that they barely count. Imports into the United States are rising, and prices have come down considerably since the first shipment of fifty boxes came in 1911, when the endives sold for one and a half good, solid, pre-World War dollars a pound retail.

Like people, some fruits are more sensuous, more beautiful and more elegant than others. Among these I would count Belgian hothouse grapes, those luscious bunches which may weigh as much as two pounds and more a bunch, where each berry is perfectly and evenly shaped and nearly two inches in diameter, its purple color deliciously enhanced by a delicate, pale bloom. Belgian hothouse grapes spell luxury in the romantic manner. They go in *bon voyage* baskets for first-class crossings on fabulous ocean liners, they hang over silver epergnes as centerpieces at formal dinner parties, and generous godmothers and lovers send them for Christmas presents. My cherished memories of these beauties go back to the weeks of convalescence after a serious illness, when my parents would deposit by my bedside one perfect bunch after another, each meticulously bedded in cotton batting and resting in its own white cellophane-wrapped cardboard box. I can still remember the pop of the grape as I squeezed each berry into my mouth, and the taste of the juice running over my tongue, so different from that of the open-air grapes from the family vineyards near Rome.

Belgian grapes grow in hothouses. There is nothing remarkable about that, but what is remarkable is the sheer number of hothouses. There are some 35,000 of them, on nearly 2,000 acres of ground, producing more than 28 million pounds of large, perfect table grapes a year, the year round. This concentration of glasshouses is about half an hour's drive from Brussels, through fertile, rolling countryside and on tree-shaded roads. The two main grape villages are Hoeilaart and Overijse, and to Hoeilaart I went, cherishing my nostalgia for the grapes of yesteryear. I was not disappointed.

Grape growing, like witloof growing, is a family industry where the skill is passed on from father to son. Three thousand families make their living from it, and almost all the holdings are small, using from ten to twenty greenhouses, where the father does practically all the work himself, except during the trimming season; then the bunches are thinned with scissors, and his wife helps him. Yet here the picture is changing too, moving toward big enterprises with as many as 200 and even 400 greenhouses. It is the problem of the eternal lack of labor; the young people don't want to be tied to a seven-day work week when factories offer good wages, five-day weeks, paid vacations and other benefits.

The cobbled streets of Hoeilaart make sharp corners

climbing up the little hills on which a friend and I were driving to get an over-all view. Below us, protected by woods on three sides, lay an irregular geometric pattern of greenhouses, all facing south, lying side by side like sardines. Under the spring sun, the endless glass sparkled like the waves of the ocean, dominating the landscape so that the houses and other buildings became invisible.

To go into a hothouse, we crossed the narrow cement walks which run like little lanes beween the hothouses. A narrow-gauge track is built into them to carry the wagonloads of manure the vines need for nourishment. The hothouse itself came as an extraordinary experience. The first and lasting impression was being in a warm, green underwater world where the watery, suffused light shone from above through the giant grape leaves that had flattened themselves against the glass in their search for the sun. A poem that I had long ago learned in school came to my mind, from Milton's *Comus:* "Sabrina fair,/Listen where thou art sitting/Under the glassy, cool, translucent wave." The grapes hung in thick and heavy bunches on the branches, surprisingly even in size, on either side of the center path of the hothouse. I was told that it was 75 feet long, 20 feet wide and 9 feet high, kept at a temperature of 70 degrees provided by pipes that run down either side of the house, coming from a central heating plant rather than the old method of lighting fires in each building. It was a totally controlled environment, which permitted the grower to give each bunch his undivided attention to make it perfect, because the grapes are truly groomed by the bunch. Only a certain number of bunches are allowed on each grapevine, and these are thinned out when they begin to ripen so that each bunch may achieve the wanted teardrop shape and each berry may have a chance to ripen evenly.

An older man was sitting on a stool snipping out berries with a pair of scissors, and so intense was the silence in the greenhouse that the plop made by each berry as it hit the soft earth had the sharpness of a shot.

A variety of grapes is grown in Belgian hothouses, to be ready at various times of the year, and so to catch the market in the countries where grapes ripen outdoors at their conventional times. The Leopold III, large, juicy and purple, is the typical grape from Hoeilaart. Other varieties are the Cannon Ball, about as large, and the equally delicious but less spectacular-looking white Muscat of Alexandra and the Purple Royal and Colman.

Again, as in the case of the witloof industry, commercial grape growing is barely a century old. The first hothouse went up at Hoeilaart in 1865, built by a young man called Felix Sohie, who had taken courses in horticulture and worked as a gardener in the nearby castle of Huldenberg. He invested all his savings in the project and it flourished, so that the other village people did the same, changing over from their rather impecunious trading in butter and eggs with Brussels.

Grapes and Belgian endives, fritures and frites—they all require neatness and precision. In a way, they are just another aspect of the precision with which the Flemish painters once painted their painstakingly detailed altarpieces, interiors and still-lifes and, above all, their ravishing flowers.

VIII

Beer and Spirits

THE NATIONAL DRINK of Belgium is beer, of which the citizen drinks more than anybody else in Europe: 140 liters per year per Belgian against 90 liters per Englishman and a puny 50 liters per German. Drinking beer in Belgium is as natural as breathing. But it is much more amusing to drink beer in Belgium than anywhere else because there are so many different varieties which really taste different from each other. Some of these beers are very local, limited to the town where they are brewed; the tax structure of Belgium is such that small breweries can stay alive and well, which they can't in the United States.

All Belgians are beer connoisseurs with strong feelings on the subject. And beer drinking can be made into a sport. When you ask simply for a beer, you are likely to get an export, or a stella, which is a light lager. In Brussels the most famous beer is the Geuze, so-called when bottled, whereas when on tap it is known as Lambic. Geuze-Lambic is brewed from a mixture of barley and wheat, and it can knock you in the eye. Some call it

La Mort Subite, sudden death. A sub-variety is called Kriek-Lambic, which has a flavoring of cherries added to it after fermentation. This makes it reddish, but it does not taste of cherries. In Brussels one may also refresh oneself with Faro, based on wheat, which is about a thousand years old. In Antwerp they make a special barley beer, and in Louvain, where the Peetermans was famous, they still make strong, frothy white beers. There are the Grisette from the Hainaut, the Saison from Liège and Verviers, the Guldenbiers and Diesters from Diest, the Old Beer of Hougaerde, the Kavesse of Lierre, the Uitzet of Malines, the Brown Beers of Limbourg, Malines and the Walloon country, the Duivels of Halle, the Bacchus of Ypres, the Kwak of Termonde, the Old Beer of Oudenarde, the Janverdieren of Alost, the beer of Orval, the Triple Beer of Ghent as well as the Drydraet of Waes. And these are just a few among the survivors of the white, black and red beers that once were brewed all over the country.

All you have to do to know that beer is the life blood of Belgian drinking is to look at Brueghel's pictures and at all the other fairs painted by the Flemish painters. The importance of the brewer's art and the influence of the brewers' guilds can be seen best in the magnificent guild-house on the Grand' Place in Brussels. This splendid and ornate Flemish Renaissance building has a little museum which tells you as much—or, at any rate, which told me as much as I wanted to know about Belgian brewing. I went to a party there which celebrated a new member who had just been received into the Brewers' Guild. The brewers and their wives, all looking remarkably prosperous and handsome, were charming; their international connections, such as breweries in Indonesia and Pakistan, impressed me no end.

The places to drink beer in Belgium are the *estaminets*, the popular taverns. Hard liquor is not sold in cafés, and beer is cheap. I remember such a student tavern where boys and girls, some in their mid-teens, sat together in utter decorum. A few of the boys had long hair, a few of the girls wore blue jeans, but in spite of their cheerfulness, they seemed, to an American, extraordinarily quiet and reserved. Most of the boys and girls nursed their beers for a long time, for Belgian students are poor. Only occasionally did one or another turn on the jukebox with rock records. And they shared the place in complete amity with a number of older men and women who did not mind the young people either.

Belgium makes a few, but not too many, spirits. The most popular is the Holland-type gin, which is strongly flavored with juniper berries and drunk straight, not used for mixed drinks as English gin is. There are also three national liqueurs: the Elixir de Spa is pine-flavored, while Walzin and Elixir d'Anvers resemble Benedictine-type liqueurs. I've been told of local fruit wines, such as cherry wines, but I have never had a chance to taste these, sticking to ordinary grape wine or to beers, like the majority of Belgians. Finally, there is the excellent cider, both soft and hard, as indigenous to Belgium as the painters who glorified it many centuries ago.

IX

Random Travels, Random Notes

THESE NOTES are meant to be a backdrop, to make the rest of this book more intelligible, and are largely about places not well known to Americans. Alas, they have to be sporadic, since this is a cookbook and not a travel book. In no way do my words do justice to the many beautiful and interesting things to see in Belgium, where the very old and very new are warp and woof of the same country. The art treasures of Belgium are incomparable: Gothic town halls and sculptures, Romanesque churches, gilded Renaissance mansions, paintings, the art of the goldsmith and the metal forgers, tapestries, glassware, marionettes that are sculpture, and finally the towns, big and small, treasures themselves, which house these treasures. But whether artistic pleasures are taken in big or small doses, willingly or reluctantly, invariably they end in beautiful meals in the excellent restaurants that exist in all parts of Belgium. Here I would like to say that very good tourist literature and information concerning every phase of Belgian life, from cities and folk festivals to shopping and restaurant guides, can be had for the asking from the Belgian National Tourist Office, 589 Fifth Avenue, New York City, or from the Tourist Offices which are found in all Belgian cities.

The "we" in the following pages refers to a young friend, Jean-Jacques Baffrey, who was kind enough to drive me around Belgium.

In the North

This cloudswept Flemish land, shaped by adversity and ravaged by wars throughout the centuries, is indeed the phoenix personified. After each catastrophe the country is reborn. Where the sea roared, land has been drained and created; where the cities were razed, they were rebuilt, true to what they had been and more beautiful than before.

The Flanders landscape is, to me, unbelievably flat and solid. On the intensively green fields, solid brown and white cows look mildly at the streamlined factories that sit around. The road takes us past the barge-laden canals that are the arteries in the body of this country. Small paths run along their high, grassy banks, and the wind-blown poplars, all equally tall (how is this achieved?) and all leaning away from the wind in the same direction, are as I thought Flanders would be. But the windmills have all gone and the country is getting crowded. Next to the low-lying gray and rather small but solid peasant houses which show a blind face to the road are the new houses of the country people, solid red brick, two stories high, with picture windows, each looking different from the other. No development housing here in Flanders. Few flowers grow in the tiny, stark gardens, but the picture windows are lined with the national Belgian house plant, the long-leaved, spiky Sansevieria, which the Flemish call Woman's Tongue. These plants, more virtuous than beautiful, sit in their white cache-pots next to each other on the window sills, commingling the joys of indoor gardening with the intensive privacy Belgians like in their homes. Net or lace curtains flutter above the top spikes of this useful plant, so that the outside world is indeed screened out.

Belgium's North Sea coast is not for those who seek solitude. On forty-five short miles, eighteen resorts melt into one another along wide waterfront promenades. Some resorts are elegant, such as Knokke-Le Zoute; others given to earthier seaside pleasures along the piers, as in Ostend. Others again are family places, such as St. Idesbald. What seems strange is that serious shipping and fishing go on among the wealth of casinos, beach umbrellas, windbreaks, dance halls, night clubs, car rallies, battles of flowers, donkey and pony rides, *haute couture* shows, tennis, miniature golf, horse racing, children's amusement parks and physical culture galore, as well as the *friture*, mussel and oyster stands and all the other eating places of a vacation area concentrated to the *n*th degree. Behind the dunes, luxurious villas in shaded and manicured gardens are the relics of La Belle Epoque, as are the formal casino-kursaals. On the beaches, when the tide is low, you can wade out a long way, and the soles and the flounders jump out of the tidal pools, splashing at your legs. What surprised me was that the North Sea waves are not as fierce as those on our Cape Cod shores. And shades of the past: there were bathing machines on the sands, little houses on two big wheels that are pulled into low tides by patient horses so that the bathers won't have to walk out for their dip and swim. It was hard to imagine bikini-ed girls stepping down the bathing machine's steps into the water, the whole thing is so turn-of-the-century.

After the apartment house after apartment house after villa after villa of this coastal strip the great bird sanctuary at the estuary of the Zwin River is indeed a breath of open air. In the 300-acre park of a former royal villa there are vast aviaries, constructed so as to imitate nature, and indeed they do. In them, hundreds of birds summer —sparrows and curlews, linnets, owls, teals, thrushes, bitterns, warblers, finches, tits, pheasant, blackbirds and even flamingoes, unafraid of humans, and even mingling with them. As I walked up to a dike, to look at the big sand dunes that hide the sea and lead into Holland, the tidal marsh was bordered with the mauve flowers of the sea lavender, and in the sky the air was thick with the brushing of wings in flight. I dined in the restaurant deep in the park, behind great tubs of deliriously flowering begonias and fuchsias. Below them, on the lawn, ducks, flamingoes and a couple of bunnies followed the meal with great interest. This was my first acquaintance with hop sprouts, which resemble bean sprouts but taste rather more like a cross of asparagus and oyster plant. They were bathed in cream and topped by a poached egg which, in turn, was topped by a *Hollandaise* sauce, the whole deliciously spring-like and squishy. The grilled turbot persuaded me once more that turbot, not gray sole, is the king of fish. I drank Sancerre with my dinner, but my companion, who chose kidneys in Madeira sauce, with green beans and *frites,* preferred beer to wine, as many Belgians do.

From here we drove through the *polders,* the land reclaimed from the sea, on our way to Bruges. Here I suddenly saw the real Flanders, a poetic Flanders, a Flanders not yet filled with solid houses and solid modern factories put there by international capital. Here was solitude—a great windswept evening sky, distant church spires, slow canals outlined in the sky by the slanting poplars along their grassy dikes, very green meadows, small drainage canals where the cows gazed at their solid images, and low farms that face the canals rather than the roads. This is a somber landscape, and when you are a part of it, on the road that runs along the poplar-lined canals that fade into the horizon, you can understand why the people need the frenzy of their carnivals, their *kermesses* and their religious processions. We passed through Furnes, the most Spanish of the old Flemish cities. As in all of them, the heart of the town is the Grote Markt, the big market, and like every Grote Markt, it is an enormous square. That day it was filled with cars rather than with market stalls. The buildings were wonderful: the stark Gothic Spanish Officers' House (1448) and the exuberant Renaissance structures, the old Boucherie, the butchers' guildhouse (1615), the Law Courts (1613), the Town Hall (1612), the Falconers' House (1624), brought home how richly, how splendidly life was lived in these wealthy merchant towns.

As in all of Flanders, religion runs deep in Furnes. In Ste. Walburge, begun in 1230 and finished around 1900, the fragment of the True Cross which Robert II of Jerusalem brought back inspires a number of processions in honor of the Holy Cross. The strangest of these is that of the Penitentes, who, robed and hooded (but for two slits for the eyes, their faces are totally hidden), carry crosses. That of Our Lord weighs nearly ninety pounds, the others around fifty pounds. As in Spain, they drag their crosses in procession, and other groups act out the passion of Our Lord. I did not see it, but this procession is said to be one of the most impressive religious events in a country which boasts very many. Among these is the Procession of the Holy Blood in Bruges, the reason for my being on the road at this time.

Bruges

Spring had exploded in the gardens of Bruges. The petals of the apple, cherry and pear trees fluttered down on mossy green roofs and gray garden walls, and the tender young green of the willows hung over the limpid canal waters. Old women were selling large sheafs of daffodils and tulips, and the potted house plants, the Sansevieria and Crassula, sat on the front steps of their homes soaking in the spring sun. Bruges was indeed *une ville en fleur.*

This lovely city is hard to describe. It has been likened to Venice because of its double belt of canals, crossed by a hundred small bridges. But Bruges is not a watery town; her canals are far fewer and wider than the capriciously meandering canals of Venice, which are indeed the city's streets. In Bruges the canals were the business roads that moved the city's commerce to the sea when it was one of the major cities of the Hanseatic League from the thirteenth to the sixteenth century. Once, more than 150 ships made their way along the canals to the city's docks, piling them high with wool from England, furs and amber from Russia, timber from Scandinavia, fabrics from Italy, oil and fruit from Spain, wine from the Rhine, and spices and carpets from the Orient. The riches of the world came to Bruges, which was made even richer by the trading of the famous cloth of Flanders, the cloth that was the cornerstone of Flemish wealth. But in the sixteenth century the decline set in. The estuary of the River Zwin silted and sanded up, closing beyond redemption even the foreports of the city, leaving Bruges landlocked. The demand for Flemish cloth fell, and, furthermore, the proud merchants of Bruges paid hard for their pride. In order to protect the home industry against competition, Bruges had forbidden the importation of English cloth. Without hesitation, the English merchants went to Antwerp, which accepted them with open arms and great privileges that were soon extended to German and Italian traders. This was the beginning of Antwerp's rise, which continues so spectacularly in our day.

Until the nineteenth century, and until the creation of a new seaport for Bruges—Zeebruges: that is, Bruges-on-the-Sea—the town lay asleep. And to this sleep the town owes its unspoiled beauty, the perfect preservation of the glorious red and gray high dormered or gabled houses which stand flush with the narrow streets. Better still, no superhighways lead through Bruges, nor do high-rise buildings mar the low skyline. Yet Bruges is not all medieval cobbled streets and palaces, churches, hospitals, soaring spires and steep, knife-sharp tiled roofs. Along canals and tree-lined squares are the charming low classical façades of the row houses of the late eighteenth and early nineteenth centuries, white, gray, washed-out blue and even faintly pink, which speak of a remembered, humbler, but most immediate past.

On the day of the Procession of the Holy Blood, which had brought us to Bruges, the town was ready for the great event of the year. The streets of the inner city had been closed to cars, the Grote Markt was filled with bleachers, banners and flags hung from all the houses.

Thousands of pilgrims and sightseers had come, leaving their buses behind them, crowding the cafés and restaurants and eating the *friture* stands bare. The mood was festive but quiet, because, however colorful a spectacle, this was a religious event. The relic, a vial containing a few drops of Our Lord's Blood that had been gathered from his wounds by Joseph of Arimathea, had been brought back from the Holy Land after the Second Crusade, around 1150, by Thierry of Alsace, Count of Flanders. The relic has its own sumptuous twelfth-century sanctuary near the Town Hall, which is not the largest, but the most elegant of all the medieval town halls of Belgium I have seen; it is stylish indeed. But on this processional day, fixed by tradition to be the first Monday after May 2, the relic was to be carried around the town in a medieval fresco made mobile, in which the actors were the citizens of Bruges.

The players were being costumed in the Halles, the thirteenth-century market building on the Grote Markt, under the great octagonal tower where hangs the biggest and one of the most famous of Belgian carillons. There was a great coming and going of old and young colorfully costumed personages on the stairs of the Halles—helmeted Roman soldiers, medieval pages, wimpled maidens, sandaled shepherd boys, folklore matrons, medieval burghers and amorphous long-gowned male and female persons carrying large bundles of palm fronds. Central casting was taking place in the enormous first-floor hall, where the costumes had been sorted into big bundles from which the participants chose their right sizes. The costumes looked extremely clean and well made, good foils for the rich silks and velvets worn by the major personages in the procession.

The crowds were getting even thicker as we went to

the seats that had been given us on the second floor of a house that lay on the procession's route. Below us, lined up along the canal, were groups of countrified men and women under the guidance of their priests, contrasting in appearance, but not in spirit, with the citified teen-agers and their parents who had the foresight to rent chairs along the route.

The procession was a series of walking tableaux in which scenes from the Old and the New Testaments were being acted out, either on floats carrying sacred statues or simply in the street. It is produced by the Noble Confrérie du Saint Sang, an ancient brotherhood (and one of the noblest ones) that sticks to tradition, yet introduces each year some little changes to prevent making the great event look outdated. That year they had mounted a loudspeaker in each float, which, in stylized Flemish and French, recited that particular tableau's meaning and gave out suitable music, heightening the dramatic effect.

The procession started with trumpet blasts from the mounted police, the Boy Scouts' band and from mounted trumpeters who were carrying the lovely old town banners, in themselves a history of Bruges. It was quite impossible to take in all the tableaux, there were so many, with thousands of people of all ages. Among them I remember Adam and Eve, in rags, on a float, crouching dejected and cast out below a splendid angel who, sword in hand, stood on a separate platform which was held up by demons. They were followed on foot by ragged, long-haired boys and girls dressed in sackcloth: the cast-outs from Paradise. Cain's face was a bloody red mask, whereas Abel was white all over. Joseph's story was a big one, acted out by Joseph and his brethren and Pharaoh. To show the Pharaoh Joseph's strength, one of his brethren flexed his arms and lifted his legs, while Joseph was trying to run away as Pharaoh looked on. The Paschal Lamb was carried by Assyrians; a statue of the Virgin in white and blue, standing on the globe of the world, was carried by men dressed all in gold and surrounded by medieval maidens strewing flowers. All the while, parade marshals, dressed as medieval burghers, were walking up and down, walkie-talkies in hand, alongside doctors and nurses with first-aid kits. I think that the spectators were far more reverent than many of the participants in the procession. Since each tableau was linked to the next one by miscellaneously costumed followers, there was quite a lot of good-natured chatting among them, hardly surprising since the Holy Blood Procession is indeed *déjà vu* to the citizens of Bruges.

The second part of the Procession, under the theme of "Behold His Body, Behold His Blood" as against the preceding "Prophets of the Holy Blood," was even more colorful, if that were possible. The Nativity float, reproducing a Flemish picture, was followed by a crowd of motley shepherds with staffs. One old shepherd was in medieval costume, with a full complement of medals on his chest. The three Kings from the Orient, one of them black, preceded the Flight into Egypt, where the blue-coated Virgin rode on a donkey, sheltering a baby doll in her arms, with a bent and tired St. Joseph at her side. Then came the forerunners of the Passion: Jesus dressed in white and brown, walking, or riding on a donkey into Jerusalem, flanked by his Apostles; the Last Supper, a most impressive float where Judas, alone dressed in black among the white-robed other Apostles, refused to drink from the chalice; Jesus, crowned with thorns and carrying the cross, walking along with Mary and John, to the rhythmic marching of the Roman soldiers that surrounded them. Finally, the Passion itself was represented by an enormous wooden statue, which was pushed along by laughing Jewish and Roman youths, while mourning girls linked their arms to support themselves in their very visible grief. The hooded Penitentes followed, carrying an extremely realistic statue of the Descent from the Cross, while other Penitentes danced ritually to an impressively sung dirge.

Finally, we came to the third and perhaps crucial part of the Procession, dedicated to "The Devotion to the Holy Blood." Here we saw richly dressed Crusaders on their splendidly caparisoned horses, alongside their plain followers, who were dragging their feet. They came in the train of Count Thierry of Alsace and his wife, both magnificent indeed. Their chaplain, dressed in black and white, made a handsome contrast. Count Thierry was presenting the Holy Relic to the city of Bruges, symbolized by joyous male, female and child burghers, dressed in Renaissance robes rather than in the medieval clothes of 1150, when the event took place. The relic itself was preceded by its own spiritual honor guard, consisting of a number of magnificent gold and silver reliquaries carried high on clerical shoulders. Then came the human guard of honor, impressive beyond description. First, the members of various religious orders came by, followed by the parish priests, the seminarians, the high clergy of the cathedral of Bruges, numerous bishops, the cardinal primate of Belgium, who all surrounded the relic in its golden shrine held high above the crowd. Alongside were the members of the Noble Confraternity of the Holy Blood, the whole city council of Bruges, and the mayor, all velvety robes and berets and golden chains, the flags of Bruges and its most splendid policemen. As the relic came by, almost all of the spectators fell on their

(77)

knees, praying, in complete silence. All the church bells in town and the carillon were peeling at full strength.

This was Flemish painting come to life, down to the last maiden carrying palm fronds. And in spite of all the gorgeous costuming, masking and pageantry bursting with color, the parade marshals, the nurses and doctors, and, finally, the thousands of tourists, there was no mistaking the mysticism of the Flemish people, or that this was a religious event, not a carnival or kermesse.

Antwerp

In this rich and beautiful city, my hostess was Mevrouw Goris, whose large house is crammed with beautiful old things, and who is an accomplished gardener. As we wandered along the neat gravel paths, she picked a few tiny flowers here and there, white and blue violets, grape hyacinths, scilla, apple blossom and forsythia. Without paying any special attention, and as we went on talking, she fashioned me the most exquisite little nosegay I've ever seen, straight out of Van Eyck. And in her house the flower arrangements were exquisite. Flower arranging, at least to the ladies of Antwerp, is as natural as breathing. So is the constant sending of flowers as social currency. Dinner invitations may bring forth only a few bouquets, but weddings, anniversaries, first communions blanket the houses in blooms. And a man from Antwerp who had lived in Chicago in the gangster years told me that a good high-class Flemish funeral compared favorably in flowers with those of the honored lords of the underworld.

Equally natural is the Flemish love for pictures. All Belgians are made for paintings, but here in Antwerp it seems to go even further. My hostess, not entirely as a joke, inquired why her husband had not bought her this or that picture at a recent auction. Catalogues were brought out at dinner tables, with such professional discussion of merit and price that it left me speechless. And this passion for art possesses very young couples as well. In spite of the great and prevailing love for antiques, Belgians love and buy most modern, *avant-garde* pictures, several steps beyond the great Magritte. Van Tourenhout is such a painter, and in one Belgian home I know, he coexists, and extremely well, with Empire and Louis XV furniture. Indeed, the old Flemish tradition of patronizing the painters is alive and well in Antwerp.

For centuries, riches have been pouring into Antwerp and riches are pouring in today. They come from the port, the fourth largest in the world, and from industry, much of it American-owned, which is taking over Flanders. Riches built the Cathedral of Our Lady, whose sensational proportions (a nave 380 feet long, seven parallel naves and 126 pillars which separate them) are so harmonious that, as in St. Peter in Rome, you don't realize the size of the place, nor the height of the 400-foot tower. Inside, Rubens' masterpiece, the *Ascension*, above the main altar, is so enormous a picture that you can see it from the front door.

Antwerp is a city of the north, of half-tints, and it is a breathtaking city. Of all the big business cities of the Continent, it is the one where the past is still alive and all tangled up in the Gothic, Renaissance, Baroque and nineteenth century to make modern Belgium. For this reason, Antwerp's smaller museums—housed in houses, so to speak, rather than in museum buildings—come alive in an extraordinarily vivid manner. Rubens' house is the most spectacular of these, an Italian Renaissance *palazzo*

scaled down to villa proportions, but with all the trim-
mings of the period, so different from the traditional
gabled and dormered northern Gothic and Renaissance
mansions of the town. Rubens' house—much of it a
reconstruction, though a most faithful one—gives one an
incredible close impression of how the painter lived and
worked, in seventeenth-century splendor, because the
seventeenth century and its splendor are still part of the
street life outside. The best of Rubens' paintings are not
in Antwerp. But none of these will give you the feeling
of immediacy, the fusion of art and life that you get
from his house.

The Rubens house is not the only one that brings such
vivid connections with the past. In the Plantin Moretus
Museum, you're in the house of the greatest printer in
Europe in the sixteenth century. Plantin had twenty-two
presses, an enormous number for the time, and he
printed fifty to sixty books a year, which were the admi-
ration of the civilized men of the time. And in the Musée
Mayer van den Bergh—this time a Gothic, not a Renaissance, house—you can see Brueghel's *Dulle Griet*, trans-
lated as *Mad Meg*, the terrifying head of a woman sym-
bolizing the horrors of war, a poor soul who is thick in
the head rather than mad, and indeed the symbol of the
stupidity of war.

Then there are the exuberant Baroque churches of
Antwerp and, even stranger to a stranger, the innumera-
ble statues of the Virgin fixed to the corners or the
parapets of houses, with their lanterns hung from lacy
wrought-iron fixtures. There are said to be 300 of them.
The loveliest ones date from the seventeenth and eighteenth centuries, the results of competitions of local artists, who then gave their masterworks to their own
neighborhoods.

Indeed, the continuity of the past has never been broken in Antwerp. This includes the language—especially the language. You don't hear a word of French, and rare is the bilingual sign, but then, French-speaking Belgium ignores Flemish in the same way. And, as in all of Flanders, you see the faces of Memling and Van Eyck, Brueghel, Rubens and Van Dyck in the Flemish of today, in a way that is uncanny.

In the South

We are driving south through rolling apple and cherry country, through an unforgettable sea of pink and white blossom all the more vivid against the green, green spring grass. The red brick villages, strung along the road, are solid, and so are the anything but quaint farms, their solid red brick picked out with a little white trimming. As in New England, the barns are part of the house. A ravishing and romantic sight that you see often, in the middle of nowhere, is a big, dreamy park, thick with enormous trees, hiding a Victorian villa. Who lives in them, I wonder. We are still in the Campine, Flemish-speaking country, and some of Belgium's oldest and finest art towns are in this region. In St. Trond the marvel is once more the Grote Markt, a severe and elegant mixture of medieval and Renaissance buildings, far more open and free than those of Flanders. All in all, the enormous market squares, without equal anywhere, are the surprises of Belgium, surprising also because their low skyline is not spoiled by modernistic buildings; whatever is modern is kept behind small conventional façades. The Grote Markt must be seen at night when empty of cars, or, better still, on market days. These immense squares were made for crowds; they need the color of the crowds to set off their splendid town halls, all lacy gray stone as in the towering Gothic palace in Oudenarde, or curving red and white brick in St. Trond.

Girls carrying large bundles of tall tulips wandered along the road to Tongres, literally in the shade of the overwhelming Gothic towers of Notre Dame. Market day was in full swing; dresses, blue jeans, shirts, shoes, yard goods, plastic pails, pots and pans hung from the stands or were stacked up in heaps. There was nothing picturesque or quaint about them, either; these were the things that you buy in inexpensive department stores all over the world. Before packing up their stuff and loading it on the trucks around the square, the hefty, no-nonsense market women (there seem to be few male salesmen) refreshed themselves in a café decorated with dense plastic foliage and flowers. We did the same, with strong beer and a ham sandwich on fresh dark bread, which was superlative. Thus fortified, we wandered through Belgium's oldest city, once a Roman stronghold, later embroiled for centuries in complicated wars. At the Beukenberg, a man-made hill and part of a Roman fortification, we looked at the tumuli of Julius Caesar's poor Roman legionnaires who were killed so far from home by Ambiorix, he of an ugly 1866 bronze statue in the town's Grote Markt. We admired the fountain recommended by Pliny the Elder for its therapeutic qualities, and even more, the energetic Belgians camping in their blue and yellow and red tents in the nearby grounds, regardless of the cool weather.

The shops in the cobbled streets were bright and noncommittal in a modern manner. Belgian cities may be quaint, but the Belgians are not, not at all.

As the readers of this book will have discovered by

now, I am an architecture buff, and the Gothic church of Notre Dame in Tongres came as a great joy. There is an exquisite twelfth-century Romanesque cloister to the church, and the magnificently severe dark-gray interior has miraculously escaped the dubious embellishments of later ages. On one side of the big nave an enormous bank of terraced flowering plants and vases filled with cut flowers—red, white or pink hydrangeas, tulips, lilacs and chrysanthemums—led to a wooden Gothic statue of Our Lady robed in gold, with an immense gold crown, who was holding an equally massively crowned Infant Jesus in one of her arms, as any mother would. But Our Lady and the Baby Jesus were both pitch black, and Baby Jesus was stretching out his hands to a bunch of grapes which His mother held out to him in her other hand. As we were looking at the infinitely touching and contemporary faces, women came to add more flowers to the large carpet of flowers; this was the month of May, the month of the Virgin. The most unforgettable sight, though, to me, was one of sorrow—even more, the essence of sorrow—in the stylized head and body of an eleventh-century wooden Christ hanging on His cross. Even now, when I hear of men suffering, I see the Crucifix in the hallway of Notre Dame in Tongres.

Liège

I would like to live in this vivacious city that rambles up and down the extremely steep banks of the slate-gray River Meuse. Indeed, one street up the hillside is all steps, hundreds and hundreds of them, with two handrails in the middle to hang onto. There is no room for large market squares along the winding broad river; it's all helter-skelter streets, small, flower-planted squares and highways along the Meuse, under the modern apartment houses with large picture windows. High up from the garden plateau of Cointe you can see that coal and industry have not made this city unfit for humans, as in America. The strip mills, the blast furnaces and the hill-high slag heaps around the town are humanized by a belt of flower-filled, luscious parks in and around the city, where the chestnut trees were in full bloom.

Until I went to Liège, I thought it was a Belgian Gary or Pittsburgh. Not at all. At first sight, you'd think you were in a lively French town. In spite of the nearness of the German border, and Germany's distinctive invasions in two World Wars, the town is totally, unequivocally Belgian, speaking only French or Walloon. Here is a town independent of Brussels in its cultural life, from opera, operetta and ballet to French and Walloon plays. And Liège, the home of the celebrated Belgian shotgun and all the other heavy industries, has been the home of a school of world-famous musicians which includes César Franck, Grétry and Ysaÿe the violinist.

In the Middle Ages, Liège was the bastion of civilization of all the surrounding lands, far beyond the borders of modern Belgium. An infinity of churches proclaims the might and importance of the old bishop's see (the prince-bishops governed the town until 1789), and handsome, vaguely classical town houses and their secret gardens speak of elegant, prosperous and cultured living. But in the side streets you see real workingclass men and women, though none of the slum housing of our industrial cities. The men wore caps and heavy boots, the women longish skirts and heavy blouses or sweaters. They had been shopping in the big, bright supermarkets and were carrying their purchases home in string bags. Fresh stuff, because frozen foods are far more expensive.

Liège is a city of museums, ranging from Roman antiquities, medieval reliquaries of gold and silver by famous Liège goldsmiths to a good picture gallery as well as an all-inclusive glass collection from pharaonic times to the present day; the famous Val St. Lambert glassworks are near Liège. The Musée de la Vie Wa-lonne, the folklore museum, is exceptionally rich and as exceptionally blessed with an excellent catalogue. The reproductions of breads, sweets and other foods, the butter molds, plates and kitchen utensils spoke of kinship with those of western Germany and even Switzerland; Europe, at least once, was a cultural unity. There is of course a puppet theater, for puppet theaters are the most typical entertainment of Liège. Before the First World War, thirty puppet theaters flourished in Liège; now there are only two. I did not see a show, but I saw the puppets, all heroes of the medieval legends of the Meuse, which correspond to the Arthurian ones. There are the four sons of Aymon, Genevieve of Brabant and Charle-magne, whose country this is. The puppets are large or small, depending on their historic importance; Charle-magne, dressed as a Crusader, draped in a velvet and ermine mantle, weighs more than eighty pounds and towers over his tiny archers. Each play, whether it rep-resents the Passion or contemporary comedy, is full of the barbed Liège satire, pronounced by the local wit called *Tchantchès*. The Walloon Museum has series of these Tchantchèses, costumed as country hicks, artisans, lawyers and doctors. Walloon, the language of the plays, lends itself not only to satire, but to earthy pronounce-ments, so I am told. I believe it, from seeing the faces of men and women who called to each other at one of the small street carnivals which seem even more plentiful in Liège than in Brussels.

The Walloons like the good life and they eat well. The cooking here is refined and even delicate, with its own specialties such as a white sausage, *boudin blanc;* *Écrevisses à la Liégeoise*, crayfish cooked in white wine and cream; *Rognons de Veau à la Liégeoise*, veal kidneys cooked with juniper berries; and the *Salade Liégeoise* made with green beans, onions, potatoes and bacon; as well as the *Café Liégeoise*, coffee with whipped cream. Excellent restaurants abound in this city, serving a sophisticated clientele of international businessmen. Before I wrote this, I went eeny-meeny-miney-mo about the great meals—and I deliberately say great—I've had in Belgium. The count stops at the Vieux Liège, housed in a Renaissance house above the River Meuse. The restaurant consists of a series of luxurious small antique-furnished rooms from which you can see the steamship and barge traffic of the river winding its way toward Holland. The food, like the service, was exquisite beyond description. I had a first course of wafer-thin, rosy Ardennes ham, which lay on a lace doily between an upright slice of tomato on one side and one upright slice of lemon on the other, put there for color contrast. Then came the most original and unexpectedly delicious dish I've eaten in donkeys' years, *Oie à l'Instar de Visé*, goose in the style of Visé, a neighboring town. It consists of a young goose (and it must be a young bird) poached free of all fat in a fragrant broth of wine, garlic and herbs, carved like a chicken, crumbled and fried, and served with a *Sauce Mousseline* made with eggs, melted butter and a pronounced amount of the garlic with which the bird has been cooked. I would not have believed that this rich dish would be not in the least greasy and come out as a perfect flavor combination. At the Vieux Liège, the sauced legs of the goose and slices of the breast were beautifully arranged with a garnish of tomatoes and scalloped lemon slices, again for color contrast. I finished my meal with a slice of melon. My companion ate *grives*, thrush, of which the Liégeois are very fond, cooked with bacon and juniper berries. We drank a 1959 Nuits St. Georges. The whole meal, for two, came to less than $20. In New York the equivalent would have cost no less than $50 or $60 and I know the service would not have been as exquisite.

Into the Ardennes

As we drove south from Liège, the mountain ranges got higher and the valleys deeper. Spa, whose name has become a generic term for all watering places, is rather small, in spite of its grandiose visitors from Peter the Great to the Kaiser, General Pershing and Hoover, and is not nearly as Belle Epoque as Vichy or Wiesbaden. To sleep, we went to a rural inn deep in the forest, where the air was thick with the scent of the pines, and the silence, except for an occasional distant cow bell, absolute. Supper was delicious: *marcassin*, young wild boar, pot-roasted in cream and served with *airelles*, the Belgian equivalent of cranberries but smaller and more tart, and hot applesauce. A *Baiser de Malmédy* topped off the meal, consisting of a mound of artistically whipped cream reposing on a large meringue, irresistible since the cream was so fresh. The next morning we drove up into the Fagnes, Belgium's only and nearest approach to wilderness, a *haut plateau* of windswept peat bogs and thick pine forests. The spring flowers were out in full bloom, amidst tall grasses which swayed with the wind. We drove along the rushing, boiling Amblève, which tumbles into a waterfall at Coo. The pretty rustic sight was all the more enjoyable as we saw it over a plate of fresh trout and a dish of strawberries. This is how I always will remember Belgium: the Ardennes in May sunlight streaking through the pine trees, dappled sunlight floating through the young green of the beeches, and white anemones under the trees.

Stavelot

I came to worship at the shrine of Guillaume Apollinaire, the eccentric French poet of pre-World War I years, who spent a year here as a youth, loving the Ardennes and also a local belle. My taste for his poetry, the *Alcools* and *Les Mamelles de Tirésias*, has never changed since I was in my teens. Grateful Stavelot gave him a museum, which the Guide Bleu recommends.

The rushing Amblève flows through Stavelot, which nestles in an amphitheater between the mountains. Cobbled streets lead up and down the hills of the little town. Many of the two- and three-story houses have rather elegant classical façades washed in light grays and blues, their windows trimmed in white. Other houses, of a more rural past, sport enormous barn doors. Keeping their fronts very citified, all the houses have big gardens at their back. The local ladies, in large aprons, were out in strength, making their town even shinier. All Belgian ladies are demons for order and cleanliness, but nowhere have I seen more water sloshed on the front pavement prior to scrubbing it with long-handled brushes nor windows washed with greater finicky energy. A hospital-clean butcher's shop offered, besides trading stamps, a bottle of beer for every purchase above one dollar.

The Apollinaire Museum is housed in the eighteenth-century, Frenchified town hall, reconstructed like so much of Stavelot, which suffered badly in the last war; the town was a stronghold of the Resistance. I went through the large courtyard, up a noble flight of classical steps, and here it was, a most touching assembly of souvenirs of a poet whose *avant-garde* poetry and whose later habits would certainly have astonished the people of Stavelot. His bedroom has been assembled in one of the rooms, and it is the bedroom of the poor French student of the nineties: a plain bed with a fringed woven spread, a small bedside table covered with an embroidered doily, his clay pipe and tobacco pouch, writing pad, pen and ink—this could be the first-act scenery of *Bohème*. The two rooms there at the museum give a review of the whole French *avant-garde* literary life of the first quarter of this century: pictures of Marie Laurencin, letters from Cocteau, Huysmans, drawings by Picasso, Honegger's music for the poet's lyrics and the touching photographs of his mother and brother (he was an illegitimate child), some fifty books about him, as well as his own portrait by Poullain, in which he looks as alienated as any modern youth, as indeed he was.

But Stavelot offered more surprises. Under the wedding banns posted in the yard hung a notice for a painting exhibition in another wing of the town hall. Past an extremely modern metal sculpture with built-in electric lights, there was an exhibition of some sixty contemporary French and Belgian paintings, organized by the Ministry of Culture of France and the curator of the local museum. Ensor, Magritte, Van Anderlecht, Rik Wouters, Alechinsky, Delvaux and many others were represented to give an excellent and quite complete idea of what contemporary Belgian and French painting is like. Stavelot is the art city of the Ardennes; the summer music festival enjoys a European reputation for serious music. The local people themselves are given to high-brow literary discussion groups, as well as to a remarkable mid-lenten carnival run by the Blanc Moussi, societies whose members dress in what looks like a take-off of the Penitentes—white sheets over white trousers, white hoods and masks with long, pointed, red-tipped noses.

Perhaps even more extraordinary than the exhibition itself was the fact that several groups of very rural schoolchildren in their early teens were being taken around by their teachers. Rather than fussing and fretting, those boys and girls kept extremely quiet and attentive, listening to every word of their voluble teachers. I listened with them, and profited greatly from the lecture.

In a small hotel facing the enormous tower which is about all that is left of a famous ancient abbey, we ate a delicious lunch of blue trout from the Amblève. A priest at a nearby table, also deep in blue trout, recommended that we see the famous reliquary of St. Remacle, a Benedictine monk who founded the abbey, and thus also the city, in 648 A.D. Outside the church, a group of rather rustic seven- and eight-year-olds were fooling around before surging in for their catechism. They were very polite, letting me pass through them with a "*Passez bien, Madame.*" Inside, a no-nonsense Father sat them down firmly in the pews. He asked the questions, and in unison they sang the answers. One boy who kept his mouth shut got singled out with a sarcastic question of the Belgian equivalent of whether the cat had got his tongue. Finally a lame sacristan let us into the strongroom which houses the precious objects. But before he unlocked the door, he asked us to read the following, on a card that he held before our eyes: "*Do not forget that you are looking at very precious treasures, which contain holy relics which are even more precious.*"

The *chasse*, or reliquary, a master product of the goldsmiths of Liège of the thirteenth century, is made in the shape of a brass sarcophagus more than six feet long, which is enormous for the purpose. Every inch of it is enameled, sculptured, jeweled, decorated with statues of the apostles and St. Remacle and other saints, as well as a triumphantly enthroned Christ and an equally triumphant Virgin who offers fruit to the Infant in her arms. On the steep roof there are scenes from the New Testament and decorations as thick and gorgeous as art can make them. There are other reliquaries in this vault, such as the ornate bust of a saint with the improbable name of Poppon; the holy man had enormous round black eyes. I thought that of all the art works of the distant past, reliquaries are most distant from the taste of our age. It takes a lot of getting used to all the chasing, carving, bejeweling, piling with statues, *bas-relief* and *haut-relief* that are part of a good reliquary. But once you have seen the point, as I did in Stavelot, there is nothing to match it for a *tour de force* of concentrated beauty.

In the Ardennes

One thinks of the Ardennes as one vast forest, but there are glades and windswept plateaus and streams rushing over rocks and boulders. The valleys of the Amblève, the Ourthe and the Semois are very deep; you look straight down on them as they meander about between the green banks thick with yellow dandelions and the vivid tents and the canoes of the campers. The houses in the stark gray villages and the farmhouses are very large, three and four stories high, gray and roofed with slate; their barns are attached, because the winter cold is cruel. On the whole, the Ardennes looks like a wilder, craggier Connecticut or like Vermont, without pronounced mountain peaks rising from the rounded ranges. This is tourist country, but the tourists have not spoiled the romance. For it *is* romantic, all legends and castles. The four sons of Aymon hunted here, the beautiful Mélusine wept her tears over her mortal husband, and Charlemagne ran after the stag with his Franks.

In the villages the butcher shops were filled with artistically displayed hams and sausages which are the specialty of the region; no tourist would leave without his *Collier d'Ardennes,* a necklace of sausage links.

We went to lunch at the L'Air Pur, one of Belgium's famous hotel restaurants in La Roche-en-Ardennes; Michelin starred it, and rightly so, as experience proved. Several valleys meet at La Roche, a tourist town wedged between the banks of the River Ourthe in a theatrical manner. The hotel sits outside the town on a ledge above the valley. The place looked pleasantly middle-class: a terrace thick with flowering plants, a salon with a picture window, a restaurant with pleasantly secluded tables, nothing fancy but the food. The *patron* and *patronne* were young and their food superlative. We started with four *pâtés,* one of veal, one of duck, one *en croûte* of ham and chicken livers and one simply called *maison,* which I thought was pork liver. Each was perfect, and very beautifully made, with symmetrical patterns of meat, truffles and pistachios, and not a speck of grease. With the *pâtés* came thick hot toast, the right thing to eat them with. The next dish was a sensational

Trout en Papillote, which had been stuffed with seven
herbs. I tasted tarragon, chervil and a bit of sage; alas, the
young *patron* would not disclose the others. A little
lemon sherbet flavored with Kirsch cleared our palate
next. The main course was a delicious *Poularde de Bruxelles*, steamed in Champagne, decorated with mushroom
caps, and with a sauce of its own juices thickened with
cream and eggs. These plump Brussels chickens are as
fine as any that ever came out of Bresse; their flesh is as
white and juicy as that of a Rubens beauty. A little
potato *soufflé* was served with the chicken, from its own
dish. The assortment of French and Belgian cheeses was
in perfect condition. The dessert consisted of a *parfait*,
made with a meringue nestling in a glazed brown *cassou-
let* bowl, which was topped with praline ice cream and
slivered almonds. It was flamed with Framboise. The
other choices on the *Menu Gastronomique* for 525
francs—that is, $10.50—were either crayfish or lobster,
Ardennes ham *en croûte*, partridges cooked in vine
leaves, or venison with its classic *Sauce Grand Veneur*,
which is made from the meat's juices, red currant jelly
and heavy cream.

Bastogne

"*La nature est en fleur*" in this lovely region, still it is
impossible to forget that the soil has been drenched in
blood. Like so many other Belgian cities, Bastogne was
almost totally demolished in the decisive Battle of the
Bulge in 1944 that turned the corner for the Allies. The
city lies on a rather bare windswept plateau, 1,500 feet
high, and in the blizzard of the battle around the belea-
guered town the inhabitants gave their sheets so that the

GI's could camouflage themselves in the snow as they organized their miraculous resistance. The town has been rebuilt, with such mementoes as the "Nuts" war museum, in honor of General McAuliffe's answer to Von Rundstedt, who asked for the Americans' surrender. A Sherman tank stands in the main square and the Café Patton is near.

We walked through the town in search of flowers to bring to Mardasson, the memorial in honor of the nearly 8,000 American soldiers who lost their lives here. Bastogne reminds one of a frontier town bustling with many comings and goings. The butcher-delicatessen shops were outstanding, and totally dedicated to triumphant displays of the products of the Ardennes pig. There were dozens of them, from the various parts of the ham to fat and lean bacon, both plain and salted, and a choice of sausages smoked either over pine, juniper or oakwood. In a café where we snacked on the "heart of Ardennes ham" sandwiches, the *patron* told us that the secret of the marvelous, individual flavor of Ardennes ham was due to the easy ways of the lady porkers. These flighty girls used to be herded in the forests along with the rest of the pig population of a village, and when the eye of the "*herdier*," the pig herdsman, was not upon them, they were not above accepting the attentions of the wild boars, their unions producing the famed Ardennes pig. As for wild boar, also in Bastogne we ate a marvelous juniper-flavored wild-boar sausage, washing it down with the powerful beer of Orval, which is made on the French-Belgian border; a single glass of it gives you a splendid kick.

The war memorial at Mardasson that commemorates the fearful battle that went on from December 16, 1944, to January 25, 1945, stands on a bare, windy mound. It is

not hard to imagine the landscape under the heavy snow
and fog of those days which worked against the Americans until, magically, it lifted to let them see the German
tanks that almost got them. The Americans used their
last ammunition and soon the Allied air force cleaned out
the enemy's positions. But Bastogne was indeed one of
the closest calls of the war.

You walk up a little path to the memorial, past some
fields where old, black-dressed women were taking in
the last hay. The memorial itself is a five-pointed gray
cement star, two or three stories high. On its walls are
the names of the units that took part in the battle; they
read like a geography of the United States. Down below,
the empty crypt is decorated with enormous mosaics by
Ferdinand Léger—the symbols of each of the three reli-
gions, Catholic, Protestant and Jewish. I pushed a large
bunch of red roses through the crypt's grille, and they
lay there like drops of blood. The very simplicity and
bareness of the silent gray memorial under a gray, wind-
blown sky can never be forgotten.

Bouillon

It is hard to say which forest is more beautiful, that of
Freyr or St. Hubert or Chiny. St. Hubert hunted among
the tall pines of the enormous forest of Freyr on that
fateful Good Friday in 683 when he held a stag at bay.
Just as he was about to kill it, the stag turned around.
Between its great antlers Hubert saw the luminous image
of Christ on the Cross, and he heard a voice reprimand-
ing him for his sacrilege on that holy day. Hubert let the
stag go, changed his heart and embraced the religious
life. Finally he became the first Bishop of Liège, and to

this day he is the patron saint of all hunters. The hunters' mass, to the sound of deep-throated hunting horns, is still celebrated in the church of the little town that is named after the saint. It is fitting that St. Hubert should have lived in what now is Belgium, for there are no more passionate hunters than the Belgians. And when you drive on the road that has been cut through the forest of Freyr's enormous trees, it is easy to believe that wild boar, hare, hart and roebuck live in the forest and are hunted now as then.

The forest of St. Hubert is somber, but the forest of Chiny was all late-afternoon sunlight streaming through the young golden-green leaves of the tall beeches. There could not be a more lyrical sight in all of Belgium at that time. It is the place to be eighteen and in love with a young poet. It seemed natural that an early traveler, Petrarch, on his way back from Liège to Avignon in 1333, wrote two sonnets praising the beauties of these forests.

As we approached Bouillon, the country became even more romantic and theatrical. We were in the country of the Semois, surely the most capricious of all rivers that ever meandered in great swooping loops between steep hills before it joins the Meuse. The best part of this lovely region is that it has not yet been industrialized at all and that, relatively, it is out of the way—down in the southernmost part of Belgium, near the French border.

Of all the lovely little towns of Belgium, Bouillon, for me, takes the crown. Like the river towns of the Rhine and the Moselle, Bouillon squeezes along the narrow banks on either side of the rushing Semois, and the newer houses climb the steep, wooded hills above the river. But one is attracted to Bouillon for much more than the scenery, for the history of this ancient town is visibly

embodied in the castle that, high on a rock, has over-
looked Bouillon for more than a thousand years.

All of the Ardennes is castle region, from Frankish
ruins to mid-nineteenth-century follies. But the castle to
end all castles is the one at Bouillon, a great fortress
which dominated the whole valley and survived seven-
teen sieges without ever being taken. The castle goes
back to the year 1000, though its exterior is quite modern
—a mere three hundred years ago Vauban, the great
military architect of Louix XIV, revamped it for more
contemporary warfare. But once you get inside, you're
back in the time when feudalism was alive and well in
Europe. The castle is long rather than wide, since it sits
on a rather narrow rocky ledge. You go through courtyard after courtyard, each accessible by low, narrow
passages that were easily held against intruders. The
walls are windowless, and sentry posts cut out of the
seeping gray stone stand on the ramparts. There are traps
in the floors, dungeons and secret passages, a chapel, and
a deep well which supplied the water. This fortress
served one purpose only: the military. There are no
women's towers, there is no room for any but soldiers on
the top of these 1,400 feet of unscalable walls.

The history of the castle is long and complicated,
since it changed hands so many times after the descend-
ants of Charlemagne built it in the first place. It was
from here that one of the castle's most illustrious owners,
Godfrey of Bouillon, took off as leader of the First
Crusade in 1097. He conquered Jerusalem, but turned
down the title of "King of Jerusalem" and called himself
"Protector of the Holy Sepulchre" instead. To finance
the expedition, Godfrey mortgaged his whole duchy and
castle to the Prince-Bishop of Liège, whose successors
held on to them for the next 600 years—to their advan-

tage, since the castle's strategic position controlled the whole long corridor which was the shortest way from the Low Countries to France.

The thing I found most extraordinary about the castle is that it makes the Crusades come alive. It is extremely difficult to imagine events like the Crusades, which took place so long ago and in such different times; I had never been able to before. But up here the mind's eye sees the Crusaders and their followers riding through the courtyards, down the hill, over the stone bridges of the Semois, through the thick, dark forests of the craggy narrow valleys and so on to the Holy Land.

We drove west from Bouillon through spectacular scenery. The road climbs high through the forests, and occasionally, far below us, we could catch a view of the Semois, whose course resembled the tracings of a seismograph during an earthquake. The high, windswept plateaus above the trees where we drove were lonely and imposing. This is rolling country, dairy country and slate country. The only sound we heard was the moo of the cows in the meadows, and the outraged moos of a herd of cows that was going home made us give way. We also met a flock of ducks driven along the road by an old woman and a very tiny girl. The farmhouses of the region stand flush on the road, like town houses. They were built from gray stone, with gray slate roofs that sloped at a steep angle. With their attached barns, they were far more imposing than the gray stone farms of Pennsylvania. Few had shade trees to soften their contours, but all the windows, whose frames were painted white to bring a little life into the great grayness of the fronts, were tightly curtained with thick muslin edged with crocheted lace.

One farm remains memorable. It was almost a stronghold, and totally surrounded by a huge hawthorn hedge that had grown to well above the house's second story, protecting it against the everlasting winds of the plateau.

The villages of the high Ardennes are equally gray and they nestle in the creases of the hills. Here the houses were softened by pear trees trained in espalier against the stone, and almost all roofs had TV antennas. The villages seemed extremely clean, and in all of them we saw men in blue smocks, berets raffishly sitting over one eye, who were sweeping the roads with brooms. The shops were surprisingly standardized and modern in these traditional surroundings; washing machines, as in America, were sold with ten pounds of detergent packed in giant plastic bottles. An old, old woman, in a polka-dotted dress topped by a shiny black apron and a cardigan sagging to legs covered with thick gray wool stockings, black wool socks and elastic-sided boots, was choosing a book from a bookmobile. And in Alle, a plateau village, where the whole church tower was encased in gray slate, we came across the rare sight of an open door. It disclosed a room almost totally filled with a wooden dresser, where clothes were drying over a stove. A tiny boy in short, short pants had come out to look over the potted house plants which filled a truck that had pulled up in front of the house. The child almost disappeared among the geraniums and begonias, the sansevierias and Chinese evergreens.

The whole region is motorized; the local rustics, men and women, old and young, go about on motorbikes, scooters and bicycles propelled by little motors; I never saw anybody walking down the road, as you do in Switzerland. The filling stations were manned by women in blue cotton uniforms who knew their business extremely well. And since this is tourist country, there was no shortage of *fritures* in the villages and even in isolated farmhouses. Oddly, besides tourism, the one industry of the region is tobacco growing; in September the fragrance of the drying leaves fills the air. Very often the tobacco planters manufacture their own cigars, cigarettes and pipe tobacco, in plugs ready to be inserted into a pipe. As for the cigarettes of the Semois, I can report that their taste is pure and strong and real.

Chimay, Dinant

This last leg of the trip seemed to be as much an exercise in eating as in cultural sightseeing. Both were delightfully combined in Chimay, which we reached by driving through a bit of France that stretches like a finger into Belgium. We followed the eccentric Semois on its way to the River Meuse, along roads hedged with hazel shrubs and beeches. The frontier is a most casual one; all we had to show were the papers of the car. But in spite of the total physical similarity of the countryside and the people, you knew at once you were not in Belgium. Admittedly, this is one of the more neglected regions of France; yet the sloppiness of the fields, the run-down aspect of the villages and farmhouses were a really striking contrast to what went on a few miles over the border into Belgium.

Back in Belgium, we went through country that reminded me of New Hampshire, a more orderly New Hampshire if that is possible.

In Chimay there is a pretty Renaissance castle right in the town, where you can see the drawing rooms of the Prince of Chimay, who still lives there. The rooms are so intimate in their rather homey splendor that I felt as if I were intruding. The castle was the home of the famous, or famed Madame Tallien, who so influenced the bloody policies of her fiery husband during the French Revolution that she was called Notre Dame du Thermidor. Her revolutionary convictions, however, did not stop her from being a society leader, and, among other things, she introduced the neo-Greek fashions of the Directoire, which worked havoc on figures not as good as hers. When Madame Tallien became tired of her husband, she divorced him to marry the Prince of Chimay and to devote herself to art in her castle. She built a charming little private theater where Cherubini, Aubert and even the great Malibran performed; today the July concerts in the same theater bring musical patrons from all over Europe.

Chimay, small as it is, is very much a town. The streets huddle together, the statue of Froissart, the historian, dominates the main square, and Madame Tallien, as she was always known, lies in the somber Gothic Eglise Collégiale.

The town seemed full of people rushing hither and yon, but nobody could tell us why. The day was cold, and we restored ourselves in a café that looked like all French cafés, but where the customers were friendly and talkative to the strangers. We had the specialties, the *Gâteau de Chimay*, which tasted like the good old four-egg cake that deserves better than the oblivion to which modern American housewives have relegated it, and *Bernardins de Chimay*, dark, sweet macaroons shaped like a tongue. The coffee was made in the most labor-saving way: a plastic filter with premeasured coffee was put on a glass, and when the water had filtered through, the filter was thrown away.

The River Meuse, as it winds its way north toward

Dinant, is the strangest river I've ever seen. It flows in a deep passage between tall cliffs, past towns and villages that follow the river, clinging to the rocks for dear life. All the time I had the feeling that I should be on top of the rocks, looking down, as you do in the Grand Canyon, rather than standing at the bottom, looking up. As I think back about this region, it is the cliffs that remain in mind. The big cliff under which we sat on a restaurant terrace, eating perch and Eel *en Escavèche*—that is, soused, jellied fish flavored with herbs. Fish *en Escavèche* is one of the specialties of the region, and since it was extremely good, I asked the *patronne* how she made it. I was in for a shock, because the whole thing came out of a can. But later on, in Namur, the Trout *en Escavèche* was home- or, rather, restaurant-made, and even better. There is nothing very original to the method: the fish is dipped in flour, sautéed in butter, and soaked in a marinade of freshly made fish stock, white wine, onions and herbs, a first course infinitely superior to any marinated herring.

The Meuse is dotted with castles and fortified farms, because there never was a time, from the Romans on, when wars were not fought here. The most astonishing and admirable example of survival is given by Dinant, a city which surely must have suffered more than any other Belgian one. It was sacked and razed in 1466 by the Duke of Burgundy, who also tied 800 of the citizens back to back and threw them into the River Meuse. The 1914 war treated Dinant no less terribly; out of the 1,375 houses of the town, 1,263 were totally destroyed. And in the Second World War the town was ravaged once more, to be built up again to look as if nothing had ever happened to it. Dinant is one long narrow street along the river, and tiny side streets under the cliffs that tower

over the city. It is a vivacious, bustling town, full of cars
and people who jam the shops. Adolphe Sax, the inven-
tor of the saxophone, was born here. There are two
specialties of Dinant: the *couques*, hard gingerbreads
baked in molds that often are wood carvings worthy of
museums, and the *dinanderies*, things made from ham-
mered and engraved copper. The art of the *dinanderies*
flourished in the thirteenth and fourteenth centuries,
when they were much sought after as far away as England. Now the craft has fallen into abuse and degener-
ated mainly into machine-made tourist souvenirs. The
shops are full of these glittering, ugly things, but occasionally you see a beautiful hand-made pot or platter. I
craved such a platter, but I could not possibly afford it.

On the other hand, the *couques* can be had in all sizes,
shaped in wondrous, fantastic molds that run the gamut
from bird and cow to griffin, Victorian valentine and
scenes from the Bible such as Adam and Eve and the
Serpent. I craved again one or two of the ancient *couque*
molds, but I could not persuade any of the *couque* bakers to sell me a mold; all they would sell was the actual
cookie. The last impression of Dinant was a splendid
cheese shop, where we bought provisions for a riverside
picnic. I remember the Franchimont, a grainy, rather
sour cream cheese, which we ate on dark bread with
plenty of pepper, and also in a buttery cheese tart. As for
Belgium's best-known cheese, the Hervé, which is moist
and yellow, I could take it with pleasure only in its first,
mild form. The medium-stage Hervé began to frighten
me, and as for the strong variety, it was beyond me. I
could well see why it had to be kept under a glass bell.

There would be so much more to tell about the Meuse
and its castles and abbeys, the famous marching societies
with their drum-and-fife corps, the little villages which

hide in the cracks of the cliffs amidst a wealth of flowers, and all the incredible, romantic history of this region throughout the centuries. And there would be so much more to say about all of Belgium. But this is a cookbook, not a travel book, so I will stop here, hoping that by now the reader will have a few impressions of what Belgium is like and why it lives and eats the way it does.

X

Appetizers and Salads

TOMATOES STUFFED WITH SHRIMP

Tomates aux Crevettes
Serves 4

This is Belgium's most popular *hors d'œuvre*, made with the country's lovely, tiny shrimp. These can be bought here, canned or bottled, imported by gourmet stores. The quantity of the shrimp used to stuff the tomatoes depends on the size of the shrimp and the tomatoes.

4 large, firm but ripe tomatoes, unpeeled
2 or more cups shrimp, depending on size
1 cup lemon mayonnaise or more, depending on taste

Salt to taste
Freshly ground pepper to taste
¼ cup minced parsley
Salad greens

Cut a slice off the top of the tomatoes and reserve. Carefully hollow out the tomatoes with a teaspoon, taking care not to break the shell. Invert the tomatoes on a plate and let them drain for 20 minutes. Combine the shrimp and ¾ cup of the mayonnaise. Sprinkle a little salt and pepper into each tomato shell and fill it with the shrimp mixture. Spoon the remaining mayonnaise on top of the shrimp and sprinkle with the parsley. Cover with the tomato tops and serve on a bed of salad greens.

Note: In Belgium, the excellence of a restaurant may be judged from this dish. An inexpensive restaurant will have more mayonnaise than shrimp in its stuffed tomatoes.

HAM HORNS WITH ASPARAGUS

Herphorentjes met Asperges
Serves 6

12 slices boiled ham	*Boston lettuce leaves*
24 cooked asparagus	*2 hard-cooked eggs, sliced*
spears	*Parsley and additional*
¾ cup mayonnaise	*mayonnaise*

On each ham slice, place 2 asparagus spears and 1 tablespoon mayonnaise. Roll up the ham, shaping it into a horn. Place the horns in a circle on a bed of lettuce leaves. Garnish with the sliced eggs, the parsley and the mayonnaise.

BELGIAN ENDIVE SANDWICHES

Tartines aux Chicons
About 2½ cups

One of the better sandwich spreads.

3 *Belgian endives*
2 *hard-cooked eggs,*
  chopped fine
½ *cup finely diced celery*
¼ *cup finely chopped*
  green onion

¼ *cup finely chopped*
  green pepper (optional)
Mayonnaise or salad
  dressing
Salt to taste
Freshly ground pepper to
  taste

Wash and dry the Belgian endives and chop them fine. Combine the Belgian endives, the eggs, the celery, the green onion, the pepper, and enough mayonnaise or salad dressing to hold the mixture together for spreading consistency. Season with salt and pepper to taste. This spread is best on whole wheat or rye bread.

GREEN BEAN AND POTATO SALAD WITH BACON

Salade Liégeoise
Serves 4 to 6

This hearty salad goes well with any cold meat.

1 *pound green beans cut*
  into 2-inch pieces
3 *large Maine-type*
  potatoes
Salt and freshly ground
  pepper to taste
1 *large onion, minced*

¼ *cup minced parsley*
1 *tablespoon butter*
½ *pound lean bacon or*
  Canadian bacon, diced
⅓ *cup wine vinegar or*
  vinegar to taste

Cook the green beans in plenty of boiling salted water until they are just tender and drain them. Cook the potatoes in their skins, peel, and slice them. Pile the beans in the middle of a large salad bowl. Arrange the potato slices in a circle around the beans. Season with salt and pepper to taste. Sprinkle both beans and potatoes with the minced onion and the parsley. Combine the butter and the diced bacon in a skillet and cook until the bacon is crisp. Pour off all but ½ cup of fat. Dribble the fat and the bacon pieces over the beans and the potatoes. Pour the vinegar into the skillet and bring it to the boiling point. Dribble the vinegar over the beans and the potatoes. Serve as is and toss the salad at the table.

Note: Vinegars vary enormously in acidity—and people have different tastes as to the right quantity of vinegar in a salad. As a general rule, it is best to start with little vinegar and add more. In the case of this salad, put a little cruet of vinegar on the table so that people may help themselves to more.

TOMATO SALAD

Salade de Tomates
Serves 4

6 firm, ripe tomatoes, peeled	1 to 2 teaspoons Dijon mustard
Salt and freshly ground pepper to taste	2 tablespoons minced onions or shallots
5 tablespoons olive oil	¼ cup minced parsley
2 tablespoons mild vinegar	¼ teaspoon ground thyme

To peel the tomatoes, plunge them into boiling water for 1 minute. Carefully remove the peel and the blossom end. Chill the tomatoes before cutting them into thin slices. Arrange the slices in a shallow dish. Combine all the other ingredients and mix them well. Sprinkle the dressing over the tomatoes and refrigerate them for 1 to 4 hours.

Note: Onion lovers may place a thin slice of onion on each tomato slice before dressing the tomatoes.

BELGIAN ENDIVE SALAD

Les Chicons en Salade

Belgian endives make ideal salads, either by themselves or added to any tossed salads, in any desired quantities. When endives are served by themselves as a salad, the leaves may be left whole, or the whole heads may be cut into ½-inch slices. For tossed salad, the Belgian endives should be sliced.

As for salad dressings, I prefer a French dressing made with lemon juice and just a touch of mustard. Chopped herbs, such as watercress, parsley, chervil, etc., add greatly to the salad dressing.

Belgian endive salads cannot be served too often since they are most refreshing and tangy.

BELGIAN ENDIVE AND BEETROOT SALAD

Les Chicons et les Betteraves en Salade
Serves 4

This is one of the best winter salads. It must be made at the last minute before serving or else the beets will tint the white Belgian endives red.

6 *large, firm Belgian* *endives*	*canned red beets,* *drained*
2 *cups sliced, cooked or*	*French dressing*

Wash and dry the Belgian endives and cut them into ½-inch slices. Put them into a salad bowl and add the beets. Toss with French dressing and serve immediately.

Note: Add 1 teaspoon of Belgian or Dijon mustard to the French dressing for this salad.

BELGIAN ENDIVE AND AVOCADO SALAD

Les Chicons et les Avocados en Salade
Serves 4

8 firm Belgian endives	*Freshly ground pepper to*
4 green onions, sliced	*taste*
⅓ cup olive oil	*2 avocados*
1 to 2 tablespoons fresh	*2 tablespoons minced*
lemon juice	*parsley*
Salt to taste	*Salad greens*

Wash and dry the Belgian endives and cut them into ½-inch slices. Put them into a salad bowl together with the green onions. Mix together the olive oil, the lemon juice, and salt and pepper to taste. Peel the avocados and remove the pits. Slice or dice the avocados and put them into the salad bowl. Pour the dressing over the salad and toss well. Serve on a bed of salad greens and sprinkle with the parsley.

BELGIAN ENDIVES FOR LOW-CALORIE APPETIZERS

Separate the leaves of several firm Belgian endives. Wash and dry them and chill them in the refrigerator. Use the leaves for any preferred dips, such as a mixture of sour cream and horseradish or lemon mayonnaise. Or spread the stem end of the leaves with herbed cottage or creamed cheese, or with a flavorful French cream cheese such as the Garlic-and-Herb Boursin.

PADSTOOLS

Paddestoelen
Serves 4 to 6

6 *hard-cooked eggs*	*parsley*
¼ *cup crumbled salmon,*	*Mayonnaise*
finely chopped shrimp	6 *Boston lettuce leaves*
or ham	3 *small ripe, red tomatoes,*
2 *tablespoons chopped*	*cut into halves crosswise*

Slice off the blunt end of the eggs and remove the egg yolks, leaving the egg white whole. Cut a thin slice from the other end of egg to allow the egg to stand straight. Mash the egg yolks and mix them with the salmon, the parsley, and enough mayonnaise to make into a thick paste. Use the mixture to stuff the eggs. Place the eggs on lettuce leaves. Scoop out the tomato halves and place them upside down on top of the eggs to resemble the top of a mushroom. Chop the egg whites trimmed from eggs and sprinkle over tomatoes.

SHRIMP CROQUETTES

Garnaal Croquetten
Serves 6

A natural favorite.

6 *tablespoons butter*
⅔ *cup flour*
2 *cups milk or light cream*
½ *cup grated Gruyère*
1 *cup minced cooked*
  shrimp
2 *egg yolks*

2 *egg whites, beaten until*
  foamy
2 *cups fine dry bread*
  crumbs
Deep fat or oil heated to
  370°F.

Melt the butter and stir in the flour. Gradually stir in the milk or cream. Cook, stirring constantly, until sauce becomes very thick. Stir in the cheese, the shrimp, and the egg yolks. Cook, stirring all the time, for another 2 minutes. Spread the mixture into an 8-inch square pan. Chill until firm. Cut it into 12 oblong pieces and shape them into croquettes. Roll the croquettes in the egg whites and then roll in the bread crumbs. Fry them in deep fat for 2 to 3 minutes or until brown. Drain on absorbent paper and serve with fried parsley sprigs.

BEEF OR TONGUE CROQUETTES

Vlees Croquetten
Serves 6

6 tablespoons butter
2 small onions, finely
  chopped
⅔ cup flour
2 cups beef bouillon
Juice of 1 lemon
2 tablespoons minced
  parsley
2 egg yolks

1 cup finely ground
  cooked beef or tongue
Salt and freshly ground
  pepper to taste
2 egg whites, beaten until
  foamy
2 cups fine dry bread
  crumbs
Deep fat or oil heated to
  370°F.

Heat the butter and sauté the onions in it until they are soft and golden. Stir in the flour. Gradually stir in the bouillon and the lemon juice. Beat in the parsley and the egg yolks. Cook, stirring constantly, until the sauce is smooth and becomes very thick. Stir in the beef and salt and pepper to taste. Spread into an 8-inch square pan. Chill until firm. Shape into 12 logs or cut into squares. Dip the croquettes into the egg whites and then roll in the bread crumbs. Fry in deep fat for 2 to 3 minutes or until brown. Drain on absorbent paper. Serve hot.

FRIED CHEESE SQUARES

Fondue Bruxelloise
Serves 6

This is a marvelous first course, and immensely popular in Belgium. My Belgian friends tell me that there is no better recipe for it, anywhere, than the one that follows. It comes from *The New York Times Cook Book*, edited by Craig Claiborne, the distinguished food editor.

4 tablespoons butter	Salt to taste
6 tablespoons flour	Freshly ground pepper to
2 cups milk	taste
¼ pound Gruyère or	3 eggs, lightly beaten
Swiss cheese, grated	2 teaspoons water
1 cup grated Parmesan	1 tablespoon peanut oil
cheese	Flour
⅛ teaspoon cayenne	3 cups (approximately)
pepper	fresh bread crumbs
¼ teaspoon nutmeg	Oil or fat heated to 360°F.
5 egg yolks	for deep-frying

Melt the butter in a large saucepan and stir in the flour, using a wire whisk. When blended and smooth, add the milk, stirring rapidly with the whisk. When the mixture is smooth and thickened, simmer over low heat for 5 minutes, stirring occasionally. Remove the sauce from the heat and stir in the Gruyère, the Parmesan, the cayenne pepper, the nutmeg, the egg yolks, and salt and pepper to taste. Return the sauce to the heat and cook, stirring constantly, until it thickens further. Do *not* boil the sauce. Remove it from the heat. Butter a 13 x 9-inch or a 9-inch square pan generously and pour the sauce into it. Spread the sauce smooth with a spatula. Cover with buttered wax paper and refrigerate overnight or longer. It will become quite firm. Cut the firm mixture into squares, rectangles, rounds, or diamond shapes. Beat the eggs until they are foamy and beat in the water, the oil, and salt and pepper to taste. Coat the croquettes on all sides with flour, dip them into the egg mixture, and shake off the excess. Finally coat the croquettes on all sides with the crumbs, tapping them lightly with the flat side of a knife so that the crumbs will adhere better. Fry the croquettes in the hot oil until golden and drain on kitchen toweling. Serve with fried parsley.

CHICKEN LIVER PÂTÉ

Pâté Liégeois
Serves 6

This is a very easy and rather delicate *pâté.*

1 *pound chicken livers*
1 *medium onion, stuck with 4 cloves*
Boiling salted water
1 *cup (2 sticks) sweet butter, at room temperature*
1 *tablespoon Belgian or Dijon mustard*
½ *teaspoon ground*

nutmeg
2 *tablespoons grated shallots or onion*
2 *tablespoons cognac*
2 *tablespoons chopped truffles (canned truffles will do)*
Salt to taste
Freshly ground pepper to taste

Put the chicken livers and the onion in a heavy saucepan. Add enough boiling salted water to cover the chicken livers generously—the amount depends on the shape and size of the saucepan. Simmer covered over low heat for about 25 minutes. Remove the onion and drain the chicken livers. Dry them thoroughly on paper towels. Push them twice through the finest blade of the meat grinder or purée them in the blender. Cream the butter thoroughly with the mustard, the nutmeg, and the grated shallots. Add the chicken livers and the cognac. Cream the mixture until it is very smooth and thoroughly blended. Stir in the truffles, and season with salt and pepper to taste. Store the *pâté* in a crock or a container with a tight cover and chill well before serving. A little *pâté* served on a couple of lettuce leaves, makes a pleasant first course. Or spread it on toast or crackers for appetizers.

FILLED PATTY SHELLS

Koninginnehapjes
Serves 4 to 8

Patty shells, made from puff pastry, can be bought in American supermarkets. Filled with a delicious, saucy mixture, they make an excellent and quite painless first course here, as in Belgium. Or else the mixture may be served over plain rice or noodles.

½ *pound lean beef,
    ground twice*
Salt to taste
*Freshly ground pepper to
    taste*
¼ *teaspoon ground
    nutmeg*
3 *cups chicken bouillon*
2 *cups finely diced cooked
    chicken, white parts
    only*
½ *pound finely diced
    smoked ham*

1 *cup sliced mushrooms,
    canned and drained, or
    fresh and sautéed in 1
    tablespoon butter*
Grated rind of 1 lemon
Juice of 1 lemon
4 *tablespoons butter*
4 *tablespoons flour*
2 *egg yolks*
¾ *cup heavy cream*
2 *tablespoons Madeira*
8 *puff paste shells, heated
    and ready for serving*

Season the ground beef with the salt, the pepper, and the nutmeg and mix thoroughly. Shape into tiny ¼- to ¾-

inch balls. Bring the chicken bouillon to the boiling point, lower the heat so that it will be simmering but not boiling. Drop the meatballs into the simmering chicken bouillon. Simmer for 5 minutes, or until the meatballs are cooked. Drain the meatballs and keep them hot. Measure 2 cups of the bouillon and reserve it. Combine the chicken, the ham, and the mushrooms. Season with the lemon rind, the lemon juice, and salt and pepper, if needed. Heat the butter, stir in the flour, and cook, stirring constantly, for about 2 minutes. Stir in the reserved 2 cups of chicken broth. Cook, stirring constantly, until the sauce is smooth and thickened. Remove from the heat. Heat the egg yolks and the cream together and stir the mixture into the sauce. Return to the heat and over low heat, stirring constantly, cook for about 2 minutes or until heated through. Do not boil. Add the chicken-ham-and-mushroom mixture and heat through, but do not boil. Remove from the heat and stir in the Maderia. Spoon the mixture into the hot patty shells and put them on a heated platter lined with a lace doily. Arrange the tiny meatballs on top of the sauce in the patty shells. Garnish with parsley sprigs and serve very hot.

BLENDER MAYONNAISE

About 1¼ cup

Making mayonnaise is second nature to Belgian women, since homemade mayonnaise is so much better than commercial mayonnaise. In a blender it takes no time at all and it never goes wrong. I use a mixture of peanut and olive oil, in equal quantities, because it makes a lighter mayonnaise than pure olive oil.

1 whole egg	*1 tablespoon lemon juice*
¼ teaspoon dry mustard	*or wine vinegar*
½ teaspoon salt	*1 cup oil*

Break the egg into the blender container. Cover and blend at high speed for 30 seconds. Add the mustard, the salt, and the lemon juice and blend 15 seconds. Uncover the jar and, blending at high speed, pour the oil into the center of the egg mixture, in a very thin stream of drops. The mayonnaise will begin to thicken after you put in about ½ cup of the oil and be thick when all the oil has gone in.

GREEN MAYONNAISE VINCENT

Sauce Vincent
About 1⅓ cups

For poached cold fish, cold seafood, and vegetable salads. The ingredients must be fresh. Use a blender.

2 tablespoons watercress, leaves only	*2 shallots, minced*
10 medium spinach leaves	*1 tablespoon lemon juice*
2 tablespoons parsley, leaves only	*1 cup homemade mayonnaise*
1 tablespoon fresh tarragon, leaves only	*2 tablespoons minced parsley*

Pound the watercress, the spinach, the parsley, the tarragon, the shallots, and the lemon juice together to make a smooth paste or blend them in a blender. Stir the mixture into the mayonnaise and blend thoroughly. Stir in the minced parsley.

(*118*)

XI

Soups

BASIC RECIPE FOR BOUILLON

Bouillon
Makes 2 quarts

This bouillon is the base for vegetable bouillon, cream soups, consommé, etc.

3 pounds shin of beef	*1 carrot, chopped*
6 two-inch chunks of	*1 leek, chopped*
marrow bone	*1 bay leaf*
4 quarts water	*½ teaspoon thyme*
3 stalks celery, chopped	*1 tablespoon salt*
1 large onion, whole	*6 peppercorns*

Combine all the ingredients in a deep kettle. Cover and bring to the boiling point. Remove the lid and skim off all the foam. When the top is clear, cover again and simmer gently for about 3 hours or until the meat is very tender. While the broth is still hot, strain it to remove the meat and the vegetables. Return the broth to the kettle and simmer uncovered until it is reduced to 2 quarts.

CHICKEN BOUILLON

Kippebouillon
Serves 6 to 8

4-*pound fricassee chicken
  or fowl*
1 *tablespoon salt*
1 *bouquet garni made
  with 1 leek, 1 stalk
  celery, 1 carrot, 1 onion,
  2 bay leaves*
1 *cup chopped celery*
2 *leeks, finely chopped*

¼ *cup tomato paste
  (optional)*
½ *pound ground beef
  round or 2 cups diced
  cooked chicken*
*Salt and freshly ground
  pepper to taste*
2 *cups fine egg noodles*

In a deep kettle cover chicken with water. Add 1 tablespoon salt and the bouquet garni. Simmer covered until the chicken is tender. Remove the chicken and strain the broth through several thicknesses of cheesecloth. Add the celery, the leeks, and the tomato paste. Simmer covered until the vegetables are tender. Season the ground beef with salt and pepper. Shape into tiny meatballs and drop them into the simmering soup. Add the noodles and simmer for 5 minutes. Season with salt and pepper to taste.

VEAL STOCK

Fond Blanc
Makes about 2 to 3 quarts

It is possible to buy good canned beef and chicken bouillons, though the varieties that are very dark brown because they are excessively caramelized should be avoided; they taste like canned bouillons. But one cannot buy veal stock or bouillon, which is the best thing (better even than chicken bouillon) for delicate cream soups. Therefore it is worthwhile to make it at home, and freeze it, if so desired. Since raw veal makes a great deal of scum while cooking, and since scum is not desirable, it is best to blanch the veal and the bones before making the stock proper.

5 pounds veal bones, including knuckle, cracked	3 quarts cold water
	2 celery stalks, with tops, sliced
1 pound veal, cut into big pieces	1 medium onion
	1 carrot, sliced
4 chicken backs (optional)	1 leek, sliced (optional)
	6 parsley sprigs
	2 teaspoons salt

Cover the bones, the meat, and the chicken backs with water. Bring to the boiling point and lower heat a little, so that the water boils gently rather than violently. Boil for about 5 minutes. Drain and rinse the bones, the meat, and the chicken backs rapidly under running cold water to remove all the scum. Wipe or rinse the kettle to remove any remaining scum. Put back into the kettle the bones, the meat, and the chicken backs and add the 3 quarts of water. Bring to the boiling point and skim as needed. Reduce the heat to simmering and add the celery, the onion, the carrot, the leek, the parsley, and the salt. Simmer covered for about 4 to 5 hours. Do not let the stock boil or it will become cloudy. Strain the broth through a fine sieve lined with a triple layer of cheesecloth. Let stand for 5 minutes and then degrease it by removing the fat with a spoon first and by mopping it up with several changes of paper toweling. Or cool the stock and then chill it so that the fat will rise to the surface and be easy to remove. Store in the refrigerator, where the stock will keep for 3 or 4 days.

Note: Check the seasoning of the degreased stock. Also, if it tastes somewhat weak, boil it down to the strength desired.

BOUILLON OF TOMATOES

Tomatenbouillon
Serves 6 to 8

5 *large ripe tomatoes,*
   peeled and chopped
1 *cup sliced celery*
1 *leek, chopped*
1 *carrot, chopped*
1½ *quarts bouillon*

3 *tablespoons arrowroot*
½ *pound lean ground*
   beef round, ground 2 or
   3 times
Salt and freshly ground
   pepper to taste

Combine the tomatoes, the celery, the leek, and the carrot with 1 cup of the bouillon in a deep kettle. Simmer covered until the tomatoes and the other vegetables are tender. Press the vegetables through a strainer or food mill or purée in a blender. Add 5 cups of the bouillon to the puréed tomatoes. Mix remaining bouillon and arrowroot until they are smooth. Stir the mixture into the soup and cook, stirring constantly, until the soup thickens slightly. Season the ground beef with salt and pepper and shape it into tiny balls. Drop the meatballs into the simmering soup and simmer for 5 minutes. Season with salt and pepper to taste.

ASPARAGUS BOUILLON

Aspergebouillon
Serves 6 to 8

2 pounds fresh asparagus   Salt and freshly ground
2 quarts bouillon   pepper to taste
3 tablespoons arrowroot   Chopped parsley

Cut off the tough ends of the asparagus. Cut the remaining asparagus into ½-inch-wide crosswise slices. Put the vegetable into a deep kettle, add 2 cups of the bouillon, cover and simmer until tender. Combine 1 cup bouillon and the arrowroot and stir until the mixture is smooth. Add the remaining bouillon to the asparagus. Stir in the arrowroot mixture. Cook, stirring constantly, until the soup thickens slightly. Season with salt and pepper to taste. Garnish with chopped parsley.

SPRING SOUP

Lentesoep
Serves 6 to 8

A lovely soup indeed.

1 pound fresh peas, shelled
1 small head cauliflower, broken into small flowerets
1 pound asparagus, trimmed and cut into 1-inch lengths
1 cup chopped watercress
2 tablespoons chopped parsley or chervil
1 small head Boston lettuce, shredded
1 bunch scallions, green part only, chopped
2 quarts bouillon
1 cup raw fine egg noodles
½ pound lean ground beef round, ground twice
Salt and freshly ground pepper to taste

Combine the vegetables and 1 quart of the bouillon in a deep kettle. Simmer covered for 15 to 20 minutes or until the vegetables are tender. Add remaining bouillon and the egg noodles. Simmer uncovered until the noodles are tender. Season the ground round with salt and pepper. Shape it into tiny meatballs. Add them to the soup. Simmer for 5 minutes. Season with salt and pepper to taste.

CHERVIL SOUP

Kervelsoep
Serves 6 to 8

3 tablespoons butter
3 medium onions,
   chopped
3 leeks, chopped
3 medium potatoes, peeled
   and diced
2 quarts water
½ cup cooked rice

½ cup finely chopped
   fresh chervil or canned
   chervil
Salt and freshly ground
   pepper to taste
1 beef bouillon cube
   (optional)

Heat the butter in a deep kettle and sauté the onions and leeks in it until they are soft and golden. Add the potatoes and the water and simmer uncovered until the vegetables are tender. Purée the mixture in a blender until it is smooth. Return it to the pot and add the rice and chervil. Simmer for 5 minutes. Season with salt and pepper to taste. If desired, add the beef cube and reheat for 5 minutes.

LEEK SOUP

Preisoep
Serves 6 to 8

½ cup butter
6 leeks
3 medium potatoes, peeled
   and cubed

3 quarts boiling water
2 bay leaves
1 tablespoon salt
1 teaspoon white pepper

Heat ¼ cup of the butter in a deep kettle. Chop the green part of the leeks and sauté them until they are soft. Add the potatoes, the water, the bay leaves, and salt and pepper. Simmer uncovered for 30 minutes. Purée the mixture in a blender until it is smooth. Chop fine the white part of the leeks and sauté them in the remaining ¼ cup butter until they are golden and tender. Add to the soup and mix well.

CARROT SOUP

Wortelsoep
Serves 6 to 8

¼ cup butter
3 medium onions,
  chopped
1 leek, chopped
1 stalk celery, chopped

6 large carrots, scraped
  and diced
3 quarts boiling water
¼ cup minced parsley
Salt and freshly ground
  pepper to taste

Heat the butter in a deep kettle and sauté the onions and leek in it until they are a pale golden brown. Add the celery, the carrots, and the boiling water. Simmer uncovered for 1 hour. Purée the mixture in a blender until it is smooth. Add the parsley and reheat until bubbly. Season to taste with salt and pepper.

CARROT AND POTATO SOUP

Potage aux Carottes
Serves 6 to 8

6 big or 10 medium
   carrots, sliced
1 medium onion, sliced
3 cups water or beef or
   chicken consommé
3 medium potatoes, sliced
3 cups milk

Salt and freshly ground
   pepper to taste
1 tablespoon butter, at
   room temperature
2 tablespoons minced
   parsley

Combine the carrots, the onion, and the water in a deep
kettle. Cook covered until the carrots are half tender.
Add the potatoes and cook covered, stirring occasionally, until all the vegetables are tender. Strain the vegetables through a fine sieve or purée them in a blender. Stir
in the milk. Season with salt and pepper to taste and heat
through. Just before serving, stir in the butter and sprinkle with the parsley.

FRESH TOMATO SOUP

Tomatensoep
Serves 6 to 8

¼ cup butter
3 medium onions,
   chopped
1 stalk celery, chopped
3 medium potatoes, peeled
   and diced
2 pounds ripe tomatoes,
   quartered

1 leek, chopped
2 carrots, chopped
2 quarts boiling water
Salt and freshly ground
   pepper to taste
2 beef bouillon cubes
   (optional)

Heat the butter in a deep kettle and sauté the onions in it until they are soft. Add the remaining vegetables and sauté 10 minutes, stirring constantly. Add the boiling water and simmer uncovered for 1 hour. Press the mixture through a fine sieve or food mill. Reheat it and season to taste with salt and pepper. If desired, add 2 beef bouillon cubes and simmer until cubes are dissolved.

DRIED PEA SOUP

Droge Erwtensoep
Serves 6 to 8

1 ½ cups dried whole peas
¼ cup butter or 4 ounces
   salt pork, diced
3 medium onions,
   chopped
1 leek, chopped
1 stalk celery, chopped

3 medium potatoes, peeled
   and diced
2 quarts boiling water
1 cup milk or cream
Salt and freshly ground
   pepper to taste
2 bouillon cubes
   (*optional*)

Cover the peas with water and simmer them covered for about 1 hour, or until the peas are tender. Drain and reserve. In a deep kettle, heat the butter and sauté the salt pork until crisp. Sauté the onions, the leek, and the celery until they are soft. Add the potatoes and boiling water. Simmer covered until the vegetables are tender. Add the cooked peas and the milk. Season with salt and pepper to taste. Add the bouillon cubes, if desired, and simmer until the cubes are dissolved.

MUSHROOM CREAM SOUP

Champignonroomsoep
Serves 6 to 8

½ *cup butter*
½ *cup flour*
6 *cups chicken bouillon*
2 *cans (6 ounces each)*
   sliced mushrooms and
   their juice

2 *egg yolks*
1 *cup (½ pint) heavy*
   cream
⅓ *cup chopped parsley*
Salt and freshly ground
   pepper to taste

Melt the butter in a deep kettle and stir in the flour.
Gradually stir in the chicken bouillon, the mushrooms,
and their juice. Cook, stirring constantly, until the soup
thickens slightly. Simmer over low heat for 10 minutes.
Beat the egg yolks and the cream together until they are
smooth and well blended. Stir some of the hot soup into
the cream. Return the mixture to the soup and heat
through but do *not* boil. Add the parsley and season with
salt and pepper to taste.

CREAM OF LETTUCE SOUP

Crème de Laitue
Serves 4 to 6

2 *tablespoons butter*
1 *large head Romaine*
   lettuce, shredded
12 to 18 *green onions,*
   sliced
1½ *quarts chicken*
   bouillon

Salt and freshly ground
   pepper to taste
2 *tablespoons cornstarch*
2 *tablespoons water*
2 *egg yolks*
⅓ *cup heavy cream*
Butter-fried croutons

Combine the butter, the lettuce, and the onions in a deep kettle. Cook over medium heat, stirring occasionally, for about 5 minutes or until the lettuce is wilted. Add the bouillon and season with salt and pepper to taste. Simmer covered for 15 minutes. Mix the cornstarch with the water and stir into the soup. Cook for 5 minutes longer. Purée the soup in a blender or strain through a food mill. Beat together the egg yolks and the cream. Add a little of the hot soup to the mixture, and then return it to the remaining soup. Heat through, but do not boil. Serve hot, with the croutons.

CHERVIL CREAM SOUP

Kervelroomsoep
Serves 6 to 8

¼ *cup butter*
½ *cup flour*
2 *quarts bouillon*
¼ *cup chopped fresh*
  chervil or canned
  chervil

2 *egg yolks*
⅔ *cup heavy cream*
Salt and freshly ground
  pepper to taste

Melt the butter in a deep kettle and stir in the flour. Stir in the bouillon. Cook, stirring constantly, until the soup bubbles and thickens slightly. Add the chervil and cook uncovered for 2 minutes. Beat the egg yolks and cream together in the soup tureen. Gradually beat the hot soup into the mixture. Season with salt and pepper to taste.

A QUICK CREAM SOUP FROM THE ARDENNES

Crème Ardennaise
Serves 4

As a rule, I am not at all fond of canned soups. But here is a combination that comes off not too badly. Made with soups built up from scratch, it is of course infinitely superior.

Combine a can of cream-of-chicken soup with one of ham-flavored split-pea soup. Of course, both soups should have been diluted to the proper consistency if they are soups that need diluting. Heat the mixture and add about ⅓ cup cooked ham cut into small julienne strips and 1 tablespoon minced chervil or parsley. Serve hot.

BUTTERMILK WITH OATS SOUP

Botermelk met Mavermout
Serves 8

This is a soup for Friday, when no meat is eaten in Catholic Flanders.

2 quarts buttermilk   *¾ cup oatmeal*

Combine 1 quart of the buttermilk and the oatmeal in a deep kettle. Cook, stirring constantly, until the mixture bubbles and thickens. Stir in the remaining buttermilk. Heat up again, but only until the mixture starts to bubble.

XII

⊸◆⊷

⊸◆⊷

Fish

⊸◆⊷

WATERZOOI OF FISH

Serves 4

This is a famous fish soup from Ghent, a delicate one. It is made with freshwater fish, and best with perch, but other fish can be used.

4 tablespoons butter
2 leeks, white parts only, cut into thin rounds
1 carrot, cut into julienne strips
1 celery heart, cut into julienne strips
¼ cup minced parsley
2 pounds perch, heads,

tails, and fins trimmed off and cleaned
2 cups dry white wine
2 cups warm water
Salt and freshly ground pepper to taste
⅛ teaspoon ground nutmeg
Juice of 1 large lemon

Heat the butter in a large kettle or casserole. Cook the leeks, carrot, celery, and parsley in it until the vegetables are soft. Do not let them brown. Lay the fish on top of the vegetables. Pour the wine and the water over the fish. Add the salt, pepper, and nutmeg. Bring to the boiling point. Lower the heat to the lowest possible. Simmer covered for 25 minutes; there should be barely a bubble on the surface of the cooking liquid. Remove the fish to a tureen and keep warm in a 250°F. oven. Bring the liquid once more to the boiling point. Stir in the lemon juice. Either pour the stock as is over the fish or purée it in a blender. Serve with well-buttered brown bread.

EELS: BASIC PREPARATION

Eels are a highly appreciated delicacy in Belgium. People eat them constantly, at home and in restaurants. When Americans can be persuaded to eat eels, they like them very much. Since eels are frequently caught by private fishermen, here are instructions on how to clean and skin them. In fish shops, they come ready for cooking or the fish man will prepare them for his customers.

Eels must be skinned before cooking. To skin an eel, cut the skin around the head. With a sharp knife, cut slowly under the skin to loosen a small flap. Hold the head in one hand and grasp the skin with the other hand. Strip the skin off in one motion. It may be necessary to use a small pair of pliers to get hold of the skin. Cut off the eel's head and cut the fish into any desired lengths. Remove the intestines and wash the fish. Cut the fish into smaller pieces, according to the recipe.

The best eels are those up to 3 feet in length since they are more tender and sweeter.

EELS IN GREEN SAUCE

Anguilles au Vert
Serves 4

This is the classical and by far the favorite Belgian way
of serving eels. It is on all restaurant menus. The dish
may be eaten hot or cold, but it is at its best cold, say the
Belgians, and I agree. The fresh herbs are essential to the
proper flavor of the sauce. I realize that it is difficult to
find fresh sorrel or chervil in America, but it is worth a
try. Of course the dish can be made without these herbs
or with the canned sorrel imported from Belgium, found
in gourmet stores, but the flavor will suffer. This dish
makes an excellent hors d'oeuvre or entree for a summer
luncheon.

*2 pounds small eels,
    skinned and cut into
    2-inch pieces*
Flour
4 tablespoons butter
*1 tablespoon chopped
    onion or shallot*
*1 tablespoon chopped
    parsley*
*½ cup chopped fresh
    chervil*
¼ cup chopped sorrel

*¼ cup chopped fresh
    spinach*
¼ teaspoon ground sage
*¼ teaspoon dried or 1
    teaspoon fresh tarragon
    leaves*
1 cup dry white wine
*Salt and freshly ground
    pepper to taste*
3 egg yolks, beaten
*2 tablespoons fresh lemon
    juice*

Wash and dry the fish. Dredge the pieces in the flour,
coating them evenly, and shake off the excess flour. Heat
the butter in a heavy skillet. Cook the eels in it until they

are golden on all sides. Add all the herbs and the wine and mix thoroughly. Season with salt and pepper to taste. Simmer covered over low heat for about 10 minutes or until the eel is tender. With a slotted spoon, transfer the eel to a large earthenware, china, or glass dish. Stir the beaten egg yolks into the broth. Cook the broth over low heat, stirring constantly, until it has slightly thickened. Remove from the heat, check the seasoning, and stir in the lemon juice. Pour the sauce over the pieces of eel and chill well before serving.

STEAMED MUSSELS

Les Moules

Mussels may be steamed in plain water, but they are better when steamed as in *Moules Marinière* (page 136)—naturally, without the sauce.

Steamed *Mussels with Mustard Sauce* (page 138) are standard fare in Belgian families. A large tureen of mussels is put on the table, and in front of each diner, a small bowl with mustard sauce, to dip the mussels in. The mussels are pried loose either with a fork, or simply by using a complete, opened and emptied shell as a pincer.

In Belgium, mussels are eaten in any month but May, June, or July.

ANOTHER FLEMISH WAY OF CLEANING AND STEAMING MUSSELS

This is according to *Ons Kook Boek*, the cookbook of the Associated Farmers' Wives of Louvain.

Put the mussels into a deep kettle or a bucket. Pour

boiling water over the mussels and stir them vigorously with a stick or a paddle. Put them into another bucket. Take them out one by one and pinch each mussel between your thumb and forefinger. Mussels full of mud will open then and are to be thrown away. Scrape the shells clean with a knife and wash the mussels two or three times.

Put a little water into a deep kettle and add some coarsely chopped onion, a good deal of parsley and celery, a little salt, and a jigger of vinegar. Cover the kettle and cook until the mussels open, shaking the kettle from time to time. Serve with French-fries or bread and butter.

MUSSELS MARINIÈRE

Moules Marinière
Serves 4 to 6

2 *quarts mussels*	6 *tablespoons butter*
2 *tablespoons each:*	3 *tablespoons flour*
minced onion, minced	*Freshly ground pepper*
shallots, minced parsley,	2 *egg yolks*
and minced celery	*Juice of ½ lemon*
1 *cup dry white wine*	⅓ *cup minced parsley*

Throw away any mussels that are opened. Scrub the mussels thoroughly with a wire brush or a copper scouring pad and trim off the beards. Wash the mussels thoroughly in several changes of water to remove any sand, but do not soak them. Put the onions, shallots, parsley, and celery into a deep saucepan or kettle. Add the wine, 4 tablespoons of the butter, and a few turns of the pepper mill. Cover, bring to the boiling point, and cook for 5 minutes. Add the mussels, cover again, and bring to the boiling point. Reduce the heat, and stirring occasionally with a big wooden spoon, simmer for about 5 to 10 minutes, or until the shells have opened.

While the mussels are cooking, cream together the 2 tablespoons of the remaining butter with the flour to make the *beurre manié*. Using a slotted spoon, transfer the mussels to a heated soup tureen or a big bowl. Cover with a lid or aluminum foil and keep warm in a 200°F. oven or at the back of the stove. In a bowl, beat together the egg yolks and the lemon juice. Strain the mussel liquid into a saucepan and bring to a boil. Drop in the *beurre manié*, 1 tablespoon at a time, beating constantly and vigorously with a wire whisk until the mixture is smooth. Remove the saucepan from the heat and beat in the egg yolks and lemon juice. Pour the sauce immediately over the mussels and sprinkle with the parsley. Serve with French bread.

Note: Oyster forks are useful for picking the mussels out of their shells, but a small salad fork will also do.

MUSSELS WITH SNAIL BUTTER

Moules à l'Escargot
Serves 4

2 quarts *mussels, cooked*
à la Marinière (*page*
136)
1 cup *butter, at room*
temperature
3 tablespoons *grated*
shallots or 2 tablespoons
grated onion

1 large *garlic clove,*
mashed
2 tablespoons *minced*
parsley
Salt *and freshly ground*
pepper to taste
Coarse *salt*

Remove the mussels from their shells and reserve. Wash and dry as many half shells as there are mussels. Put a mussel in each half shell. Cream together the butter, the shallots, the garlic clove, the parsley, and salt and pepper to taste. The mixture must be very smooth. Cover each mussel with a little of the mixture and smooth it down. Cover a baking sheet or baking dish with the coarse salt. Place the shells with the mussels on the salt, making sure that they are sitting down firmly and won't overturn. Run under the broiler until the butter is melted and the mussels are heated through. Serve on hot plates, with a garnish of parsley.

Note: The cooked mussels may also be stuffed in escargot shells, in the same manner as snails. This is really a better method because the butter won't run out of a snail shell as easily as it will from a mussel shell.

MUSTARD SAUCE FOR STEAMED MUSSELS

Sauce Moutarde
About 1 ½ cups

Basically this sauce is a matter of taste, the ingredients to be adjusted to one's liking.

5 tablespoons salad oil　　*Salt and freshly ground*
3 tablespoons vinegar　　*pepper to taste*
1 teaspoon Dijon mustard
or mustard to taste

Combine all the ingredients and mix thoroughly.

BAKED EGGS AND SHRIMP

Gratin d'Oeufs du Littoral
Serves 4

A good luncheon or supper dish, and because of the mustard and shrimp, tastier than the American version.

2 tablespoons butter
2 tablespoons flour
1½ cups milk or light cream
1 to 2 tablespoons Dijon mustard
Salt and freshly ground pepper to taste
2 tablespoons minced parsley

1 cup or more (to taste) coarsely chopped shrimp (if the shrimp are tiny, leave them whole)
6 hard-cooked eggs, shelled
¼ cup grated Swiss cheese
2 tablespoons fine dry bread crumbs

Heat the butter and stir in the flour. Cook, stirring constantly, for about 1 to 2 minutes. Add the milk and cook, stirring constantly, until the mixture is smooth and thickened. Stir in the mustard and salt and pepper to taste. Add the parsley and the shrimp. Butter a shallow baking dish generously and spread a little less than half of the sauce on its bottom. Cut the eggs into halves lengthwise and arrange them on the sauce. Spoon the remaining sauce over the eggs. Combine the cheese and the bread crumbs and sprinkle them over the eggs. Run under a hot broiler until the top is brown and bubbly.

Note: Obviously this dish can be made without the shrimp. In this case, there should be more mustard in the sauce so that it won't taste flat. The mustard must be a Dijon-type mustard. English mustard is too sharp.

FILLETS OF SOLE INDIENNE

Sole à l'Indienne
Serves 4 to 6

This dish may be made with any fish fillets. If frozen fillets are used, they *must* be well thawed out, having given up all their water, and thoroughly dried on kitchen paper.

*2½ pounds skinless and
boneless fillets of sole
1½ to 2 cups heavy cream
Salt and freshly ground
pepper to taste
½ teaspoon mild curry*

*¼ pound fresh
mushrooms, caps only,
chopped extremely fine,
like cornmeal
Paprika*

Cut the fish into serving pieces. Or if the fillets are thin and small, fold them in half. Lay the fillets into a generously buttered baking dish in one slightly overlapping layer. Combine 1½ cups of the cream with salt, pepper, and the curry and mix well. Spoon the mixture over the fish, together with the mushrooms. Bring to the simmering point. Cover and simmer for about 8 to 10 minutes, depending on the thickness of the fillets. If necessary, add more cream to keep the fish barely covered. Sprinkle with paprika before serving with plain buttered rice or boiled potatoes.

Note: The curry flavor should be very faint and the mushrooms should have melted into the cream; this is the reason for chopping them so minutely.

TROUT IN ASPIC

Forel in Aspic
Serves 4 to 6

For Fish Bouillon:

6 trout

2 cups water

2 cups white wine

2 teaspoons salt

1 lemon, sliced

1 leek, sliced

1 cup sliced celery

2 bay leaves

½ teaspoon crumbled
  thyme

4 whole cloves

3 peppercorns

Aspic:

1 tablespoon unflavored
  gelatin

2 tablespoons vinegar

1¾ cups fish stock

Combine all the ingredients except those for the aspic in
a large skillet. Bring to the boiling point, lower the heat,
and simmer for 7 to 15 minutes or until the fish flakes
easily; cooking time depends on the size of the fish. Let
the trout cool in the fish stock. Place the trout in a single
layer on a platter. Reserve 1¾ cups of the fish stock.
Chill. Combine the gelatin and the vinegar. Place over
low heat and stir until the gelatin is dissolved. Stir in the
fish bouillon. Chill it until it is syrupy and the consistency of unbeaten egg whites. Spoon the gelatin over the
trout, coating them evenly. Chill until firm. Garnish
with sliced tomatoes, sliced eggs, and parsley.

SOUSED FISH

Poissons en Escabèche
Serves 6

This piquant dish may be served as an hors d'oeuvre or as the main course for lunch. It is a specialty of the Meuse region, using river fish. But saltwater fish, such as herring, pilchard, or mackerel, may be substituted. The fish must be small, and whole. As with all of these old recipes, there are various versions, some milder, some sharper, and some even thickened with gelatin, but the main thing is that the Escabèche be well flavored.

2 pounds freshwater fish, such as trout, pike, eel, carp, whitefish, perch, etc.
Freshly ground pepper
Flour
6 tablespoons olive oil or more
1 large onion, thinly sliced
1 large carrot, sliced
1 garlic clove, mashed
1 cup water

2 cups dry white wine
2 tablespoons wine vinegar
½ teaspoon ground thyme
½ teaspoon ground marjoram
2 bay leaves
3 parsley sprigs
Salt to taste
1 thinly sliced lemon
½ cup minced parsley or chervil

Wash and dry the fish thoroughly, and sprinkle it lightly with pepper. Coat the fish on all sides with flour. Heat the oil in a large, deep skillet. Sauté the fish in it until it is golden brown and flaky. Drain the fish on kitchen paper and put it into a deep serving dish. Add the remaining oil to the skillet. Cook the onion, the carrot, and garlic in it until the vegetables are almost tender. Do not brown them. Add the water, the wine, the vinegar, the thyme, marjoram, bay leaves, and parsley sprigs. Season to taste with salt. Bring to the boiling point. Lower the heat, cover and simmer for 15 minutes. Cool a little and pour over the fish. Cover and marinate in the refrigerator for 24 hours. Serve well chilled from the same dish, and decorate with lemon slices and minced parsley or chervil before serving.

XIII

Chicken and Birds

WATERZOOI OF CHICKEN

Serves 4

This is perhaps the best-known Belgian dish, originating in Flanders. Waterzooi, also made with fish or rabbit, is something between soup and stew, and served in soup plates. There are a number of different variations; what matters to me is that the soup/sauce should not be too thick. The stock in which the chicken is cooked should be very well flavored.

4 tablespoons butter
4 large leeks, white parts only, chopped
4 celery stalks, chopped
2 carrots, chopped
1 onion, chopped
3 parsley sprigs
⅛ teaspoon ground nutmeg
⅛ teaspoon ground thyme

1 bay leaf
1 4-to-5-pound roasting chicken ready to cook
6 to 8 cups well-flavored chicken bouillon or Veal Stock (page 120)
3 egg yolks
½ cup heavy cream
Juice of 1 lemon
Salt and freshly ground pepper to taste

Heat the butter in a large heavy casserole or kettle. Cook all the vegetables and herbs in it for about 5 minutes, stirring constantly, or until the vegetables are semi-soft. Do not let brown. Lay the chicken on the vegetables and pour enough bouillon over it to cover the bird. Cover, bring to the boiling point and simmer for about 45 minutes to 1 hour or until the chicken is tender. Remove the chicken from the broth and skin it. Discard the skin, cut the chicken into pieces, and bone the chicken, that is, remove the bones that are easy to remove. Keep the meat in as large pieces as possible and keep warm, in 250°F. oven. Strain the chicken broth into a saucepan. Place over high heat and reduce to 4 cups. In a heated soup tureen, beat together the egg yolks and the cream. Slowly stir in the chicken broth and the lemon juice, and season with salt and pepper to taste. Add the chicken pieces and serve immediately, with either boiled potatoes or well-buttered slices of brown bread.

VARIATION: GREEN WATERZOOI

This variation comes from the Paul Van de Velde home in Ghent, and I prefer it to the standard one. Proceed as in Waterzooi (above) through skinning, cutting up, and boning the chicken, keeping it warm. Strain the broth. Purée the vegetables from the strained broth in a blender or push through a fine sieve. Reduce the chicken broth to 4 cups. Add these 4 cups of broth to the puréed vegetables and blend well. Beat together the egg yolks and the cream and stir the liquid gradually into the mixture. Stir in the lemon juice. Add ⅓ cup minced parsley to the mixture and add the chicken.

Note: If fresh chervil is available, use ¼ cup minced fresh chervil and ¼ cup minced parsley.

(*145*)

CHICKEN FRICASSEE

Fricassee Van Kip
Serves 6 to 8

1 large fricassee or stewing chicken, cut up	*¼ cup butter*
Salt and freshly ground pepper to taste	*1 pound mushrooms, sliced*
1 pound ground lean beef, ground several times	*½ cup flour*
	2 tablespoons lemon juice
3 cups broth drained from chicken	*Patty shells, toast or potatoes*

In a deep kettle, cover the chicken with water. Add the salt and pepper to taste. Simmer covered for 1 to 1½ hours or until the chicken is tender. Drain the chicken and reserve the broth. Remove the bones and skin from the chicken. Dice the meat. Season the ground beef with salt and pepper. Shape it into tiny balls. Drop the meatballs into the simmering chicken broth. Cook until the meatballs are cooked through. Remove the balls and simmer the broth until 3 cups of broth remain. Melt the butter and sauté mushrooms until wilted. Stir in the flour. Gradually stir in the chicken broth and lemon juice. Cook over low heat stirring constantly until the sauce is smooth and thickened. Stir in the chicken and meatballs. Reheat and season to taste with salt and pepper. Spoon into patty shells or over toast or potatoes.

Note: If desired add 1 cup finely chopped smoked ham and 1 cup grated Swiss cheese to the sauce for added flavor. Stir in cheese one handful at a time until sauce is smooth and cheese melted.

CHICKEN WITH MUSHROOMS

Kip met Champignons
Serves 4

*1 three-pound chicken,
   cut into quarters
Salt and freshly ground
   pepper to taste
⅓ cup butter
2 tablespoons water
¼ pound mushrooms,
   sliced*

*2 tablespoons lemon juice
½ cup heavy cream
1 tablespoon flour mixed
   with 2 tablespoons
   water
3 tablespoons cognac
Potato croquettes, French-
   fries, or potato balls*

Sprinkle the chicken with salt and pepper. Cook the pieces in the hot butter until they brown. Add the water, cover tightly, and simmer for 45 minutes to 1 hour or until the chicken is tender. Combine the mushrooms and lemon juice. Simmer until the mushrooms are tender. Remove the chicken to a hot platter and keep warm. Stir the heavy cream into the pan drippings. Add the mushrooms, the flour mixture, and the cognac. Stir over low heat until the sauce is smooth and thickened. Spoon sauce over chicken.

CHICKEN À L'INSTAR DE VISÉ

Poulet à l'Instar de Visé
Serves 4

This dish, like the classic Goose à l'Instar de Visé (page 156), is one of the glories of Liège cooking. The sauce is the important part of the whole thing. It depends on the flavor of the bouillon and the part played by the garlic, which makes the sauce subtly aromatic, and not at all what we would call garlicky. The reason for this is that garlic, when boiled, loses its acrid taste and aftereffects to a great extent. The amount of garlic in the recipe below gives the rather light flavor which I like, but it may be increased by 2, 4, or even 6 garlic cloves. The recipe is not nearly as complicated as it looks, and, in any case, well worth the effort because the dish is delicious.

For the Broth:

12 large garlic cloves	2 cups dry white wine
2 large celery stalks, with a few leaves, chopped	1 tablespoon salt
	5 whole peppercorns
	Chicken's neck and gizzard
1 large carrot, chopped	
1 large onion, chopped	1 2½- to 3-lb. chicken, cut into quarters
5 sprigs parsley	
3 cups water	

For the Fried Chicken:

Flour	Fine dry bread crumbs
2 eggs, beaten with a little salt and freshly ground pepper	Oil or shortening for frying

For the Sauce:

The garlic cloves	5 tablespoons flour
3 egg yolks	3 cups chicken broth
⅓ cup heavy cream	Juice of 1 lemon
4 tablespoons butter	

Cut a 5-inch square from a single layer of cheesecloth. Peel the garlic cloves and tie them into the cheesecloth, fastening the bag with kitchen string. In a deep kettle combine the garlic cloves, the celery, carrot, onion, parsley, water, wine, salt, peppercorns, and the chicken's neck and gizzard. Bring to the boiling point, cover tightly, and simmer over low heat for 30 minutes. Cut any visible fat from the chicken, wash the pieces, and add them to the broth. Bring to the boiling point, lower the heat again, and simmer covered for about 35 minutes or until the chicken is tender. Do not overcook it since it has to be fried later. Remove the chicken pieces and the bag with the garlic cloves from the broth and reserve both. Drain the broth and measure it. There should be 3 cups. If there is more broth, bring it to the boiling point and reduce it to 3 cups. Degrease the broth by skimming off the fat with a spoon and by blotting it off with kitchen paper toweling. Or chill the broth and remove any fat that has risen to the top.

All of these steps can be made ahead of time. Refrigerate the food until you are ready to finish the dish, which consists of frying the chicken and making the sauce just before serving time.

To fry the chicken: Do it any favorite way, but quickly. The chicken is already cooked and only needs to be heated through and crisped to an appetizing golden-brown color. Or fry the chicken in about 2 inches of oil or shortening heated to 375°F. on the frying thermometer, or when a 1-inch cube of bread dropped into the shortening turns brown while you count to 60. Fry the chicken for about 5 or 10 minutes, turning it once. Drain it on kitchen paper toweling and keep it hot.

To make the sauce: Remove the garlic cloves from the bag, mash them and strain them through a fine sieve into a mixing bowl. Add the egg yolks and the cream and blend well together. Heat the butter in a saucepan and stir in the flour. Cook, stirring constantly, for about 2 minutes. Add the chicken broth and cook, stirring constantly, until the mixture is smooth and somewhat thickened. Lower the heat to lowest possible and cook covered, stirring frequently, for about 10 minutes. This removes the raw flavor of the flour which spoils so many sauces. Remove from the heat. Beat 1 cupful of the sauce by tablespoonfuls into the garlic mixture. Gradually beat in the remaining sauce. Pour the sauce back into the saucepan. Return to lowest possible heat, and stirring constantly, heat the sauce through without bringing it to the simmering point. Check the seasoning, and if necessary, add a little more salt and pepper. Remove from the heat and stir in the lemon juice.

Put the chicken pieces on a warm platter and dribble a little sauce on them. Serve the remaining sauce in a sauceboat. The quantities of the sauce are ample, as Belgians like sauce. Serve with boiled potatoes and a green vegetable, such as *Peas Ardennoise*.

Note: Obviously, it is possible to do this dish in a more conventional manner, by frying the chicken the usual way and by making the sauce from canned chicken broth. But the sauce will not be the same at all because the canned broth is not remotely as flavorful as the broth made as described above.

OVEN-FRIED CHICKEN

Braadkip in de Oven
Serves 4

The Belgians carve their birds and meats in the kitchen.

1 2½- to 3-pound frying chicken	¼ cup cooking oil
Salt and freshly ground pepper to taste	1 cup water
⅛ teaspoon ground nutmeg	2 teaspoons potato starch or cornstarch mixed with 2 tablespoons water
¼ cup butter	

Wash the chicken and pat it dry. Sprinkle it inside and out with salt, pepper, and nutmeg. Place the butter inside the chicken. Brush the roasting pan and the chicken with oil. Cover the chicken with buttered parchment paper. Roast in a preheated hot oven (400°F.) for 10 minutes, lower temperature to 325°F. and roast another 50 to 60 minutes or until the bird is tender. Halfway through the roasting period turn chicken and cover it with another piece of buttered parchment paper. Remove the chicken to a hot platter and keep it warm. Stir water into the pan drippings. Scrape all drippings and bring to the boiling point. Stir in the potato starch or cornstarch and cook, constantly stirring until the sauce is smooth and thickens. Season to taste with salt and pepper. Carve the chicken and spoon sauce over chicken.

CHICKEN ROASTED IN THE POT
WITH GRAVY

Gebraden Kip
Serves 4

Very good with American biscuits.

1 2½- to 3-*pound frying*   *Water*
   chicken   1 *tablespoon cornstarch*
Salt and freshly ground   *mixed with 2*
   pepper to taste   *tablespoons water*
¼ *cup butter*

Wash the chicken and pat it dry. Sprinkle the chicken
inside and out with the salt and pepper. Heat the butter
in a Dutch oven. Brown the chicken in it on all sides.
Add 2 tablespoons water. Cover tightly and simmer over
low heat for 1 to 1½ hours or until the chicken is tender.
While the chicken is cooking spoon the drippings over
the chicken 6 to 7 times. Carve the chicken, put it on a
hot platter, and keep it warm. Stir 1 cup water into the
pan drippings, scraping to loosen all particles. Stir the
cornstarch mixture into pan drippings. Cook, stirring
constantly, over low heat until the sauce thickens. Season
with salt and pepper to taste and spoon the sauce over
the chicken.

CHICKEN ROASTED WITH MUSTARD

Poulet à la Moutarde
Serves 4

Roast chicken is usually one of the blandest and dullest
of dishes when it could be a superlatively tasty one. This

is chiefly due to the quality of almost all of our chicken, assembly-line produced birds that look good but have practically no flavor, so that they have to be gussied up with all sorts of herbs, wines, and spices. The following recipe takes this into account, by coating the bird with French or Belgian mustard before roasting. The mustard, however, *must* be the imported Belgian or Dijon type; I have found no American mustard that will take their place. There will be no excessive mustard flavor in the finished bird; as a matter of fact, no mustard flavor at all, just a delicious mild spiciness which is excellent with either the hot or cold chicken.

Another reason for the miserable roast chickens which afflict our nation is that their meat is dried out, especially the breasts. This comes from the fallacious way, propagated by almost all cookbooks, of roasting the bird breast-side up. This way, the breast cooks quicker than the legs, drying out, and the juices drain into the chicken's back, the part which is not eaten. If you roast the chicken as described below, you will come up every time with a deliciously moist, tender chicken.

2½- to 3-pound chicken	*Belgian mustard or French*
Salt	*Dijon-type mustard*
	Olive oil

Preheat the oven to hot (425°F.).

Remove all excess fat from the chicken. Rub the chicken with salt inside and out and truss. Using a pastry brush, spread the chicken generously on all sides with the mustard, taking care to cover the parts under the wings and the legs. Dribble olive oil all over the chicken. Place the chicken on a rack on its side. Roast for 7 minutes, turn on the other side, and roast for another 7 minutes. Baste the chicken once for each side. Lower the

oven temperature to moderate (375°F.). Continue roasting the chicken for 15 to 20 minutes on each side, or
about 18 minutes to the pound. Baste the chicken every 7
minutes or so; continuous basting is the secret of a juicy
chicken. It should not be overcooked; the chicken is
done when the juices that run out from the inside when
the chicken is lifted are clear. If the breast does not look
properly browned, stand the chicken breast-up for the
last 10 minutes. Remove the trussing string, place the
chicken on a hot platter, carve, and serve with French-
fried potatoes and a salad of Belgian endive.

CHICKEN IN RED WINE

Coq au Vin
Serves 3 to 4

The Belgian version of a French dish.

¼ *pound lean salt pork,*
   diced
4 *tablespoons butter*
1 *3-pound chicken, cut*
   into serving pieces
12 *small white onions*
½ *pound small*
   mushrooms, caps only
1 *garlic clove, minced*

1 *tablespoon flour*
2 *cups dry red wine*
Salt and freshly ground
   pepper to taste
¼ *teaspoon ground*
   thyme
¼ *cup minced parsley*
1 *bay leaf, crumbled*
½ *cup warmed cognac*

Pour boiling water over the salt pork and let it stand for
5 minutes. Drain the pork, dry it, and reserve it. Heat 3
tablespoons of the butter in a large casserole. Brown the
chicken pieces in it on all sides. Remove the chicken
pieces to a hot platter and keep warm. Add the salt pork,

the onions, the mushrooms, and the garlic clove to the casserole. Cook over medium heat, stirring constantly, for about 3 minutes, or until the vegetables are browned. Stir in the flour. Add the wine and season with salt and pepper. Add the thyme, the parsley, and the bay leaf. Bring to the boiling point and lower the heat so that the sauce will simmer. Return the chicken pieces to the casserole and the sauce. Simmer covered over low heat for about 30 to 40 minutes or until the chicken is tender. Stir occasionally and check the moisture. If the sauce is too thick, add a little hot water; if it is too thin, cook without cover to reduce it. Before serving, stir in the remaining tablespoon of the butter and the cognac. Boiled potatoes are best with this, or noodles.

DUCK WITH ORANGE

Eend met Appelsien
Serves 4

4 navel oranges
2 tablespoons butter
1 duckling, fresh or
   frozen thawed

Salt and freshly ground
   pepper to taste
½ cup heavy cream
3 tablespoons cognac
1 tablespoon flour

Grate the rind from 4 oranges. Peel 2 of the oranges and dice the meat. Mix the rind of 2 oranges with the butter. Put the rind mixture and diced orange into the duckling. Sew or skewer the opening. Remove all excess fat from the duckling. Sprinkle the duckling with salt and pepper and rub outside with remaining orange rind. Cook in a preheated moderate oven (350°F.) for 2 to 2½ hours or until duckling is tender. Pour or spoon off the fat as it accumulates in the pan. Prick skin before roasting if a crisp skin is desired. Remove the duckling, place it on a hot platter, and keep warm. Drain off the excess fat. Squeeze the juice from 2 remaining oranges and add to pan. Boil, scraping drippings. Stir in the cream. Mix the cognac and the flour and stir into the pan. Cook over low heat, stirring constantly until sauce is smooth and thickened. Spoon the sauce over the duckling.

To garnish: Halve 4 oranges and scoop out the pulp. Dice the pulp and refill shell. Spoon orange marmalade over the pulp. Top with candied cherry and angelica. Sprinkle with confectioners' sugar and heat in a moderate oven (350°F.) for 10 to 15 minutes. Place the oranges around the duckling and garnish with watercress.

GOOSE À L'INSTAR DE VISÉ

Oie à l'Instar de Visé

This dish is the mother of the *Chicken à l'Instar de Visé* (page 147). It is prepared in the same manner. However, there is one essential point: the goose must be young, not weighing more than 4 pounds, like a large chicken. And it also must be a lean bird. Unless you have access to such a young, unfrozen goose, the dish is not worth making. I tried it with larger geese, both local New York City ones and geese imported from the Midwest, which usually are better in quality, but it did not work because the birds were too large and too fat. In roasting, the fat will come out, but not in boiling, so that the bird is no good unless it is lean. Under ideal circumstances, this is one of the best poultry dishes in the world, and worth aiming for; away from the big cities it should be possible to get a young, lean, fresh goose.

STUFFED ROAST PHEASANT

Faisan à la Flamande
Serves 2 to 4

Pheasants in full plumage are standard subjects of the
still lifes the Flemish painters painted with such exuber-
ance. To this day they are the symbol of opulent living
in Belgium. The recipe below is for a young bird that
can be roasted; older birds should be marinated and
cooked in moist heat. A young bird has short round
claws, gray legs, and a flexible breast bone. Male birds
weigh up to 5 pounds; hens, which are more tender,
from 2 to 3 pounds.

½ *pound ground veal*	*1 3- to 4-pound pheasant*
1 slice white bread,	*Thinly sliced salt pork*
without crust, crumbled	*(about 4 ounces)*
1 egg, beaten	*4 tablespoons butter*
2 tablespoons finely	*4 tablespoons water*
chopped truffles	*8 tablespoons cognac*
(canned truffles will do)	½ *to 1 cup heavy cream*
2 tablespoons minced	*2 tablespoons cornstarch*
onion	*or potato starch*
½ *teaspoon salt*	*1 pound small white*
¼ *teaspoon freshly*	*cooked onions*
ground pepper	*Poached peaches or*
¼ *teaspoon ground*	*apricots, halved*
nutmeg	

Preheat the oven to moderate (350°F.).

Combine the veal, the bread, the egg, truffles, onion,
salt, pepper, and nutmeg and mix thoroughly. Wash and

dry the pheasant inside and out and stuff it with the meat mixture. Sew or skewer the opening. Tie the legs together with string and turn the wings under. Pour boiling water over the salt pork slices, let stand for 2 minutes, drain, and dry well. Cover the breast of the bird with the salt pork slices and tie them with string. In a skillet, heat the butter and brown the pheasant in it on all sides. Transfer the pheasant to a shallow baking pan. Add the water and 4 tablespoons of the cognac. Roast for about 1 to 1½ hours or about 25 minutes to the pound or until the bird is tender, but not overcooked. Baste the bird very frequently with the pan juices. Remove the salt pork slices 15 minutes before the bird is finished to let the breast brown. Remove the pheasant to a hot platter and keep it hot. Skim the fat off the pan juices. Blend the cornstarch with ½ cup of the heavy cream. Stir the mixture, together with the remaining cognac, into the pan juices, scraping up the brown bits at the bottom of the pan. If the sauce is too thick, add more cream. Add the onions and heat through. Check the seasonings. Keep the sauce hot, but do not boil it. Carve the pheasant but leave the stuffing whole. Slice the stuffing. Arrange the pheasant pieces on the platter and put the sliced suffing around them. Spoon the sauce over the bird and the meat. Serve hot, with a garnish of poached peach or apricot halves.

PARTRIDGES COOKED WITH CABBAGE

Perdrix aux Choux
Serves 6

All game birds are good this way, a hearty one and one that makes them taste less gamy. As for juniper berries, when they are really fresh, 1 for each bird will give the right amount of taste. But since they are almost always stale when bought, their number may be increased to 2 or 3, and they should be crushed to release their flavor.

6 slices bacon
Salt and freshly ground
  pepper to taste
6 partridges, dressed and
  trussed
6 or more juniper berries,
  crushed
4 tablespoons lard or
  butter

1 medium-size green
  cabbage
Boiling water
1 large onion, minced
½ teaspoon ground
  nutmeg
¼ teaspoon ground
  thyme
1 bay leaf, crumbled
¼ cup minced parsley

Pour boiling water over the bacon slices and let them stand for 3 minutes. Drain the bacon and dry it with kitchen toweling. Rub the partridges inside and out with salt and pepper, and put 1 or more juniper berries into each bird. Tie 1 bacon slice around each bird. Heat the lard in a deep skillet which has a tight cover and brown the birds in it on all sides. Reserve the birds and the skillet and the juices in which they were cooked. Trim the coarse stalks and wilted leaves off the cabbage and cut it into 4 pieces. Put it into a saucepan, cover it with boiling water, and cook it for 5 minutes. Drain the cabbage, squeeze it dry, and shred it. Return the skillet and its juices to the heat and cook the onion in it until it is soft, but do not brown it. If the skillet should look dry and not have enough fat in it, add 1 or 2 more table-spoons lard. Scrape all the brown bits up from the bottom. Add the cabbage and season with salt, pepper, and the ground nutmeg. Cover the skillet tightly. Over the lowest possible heat, stirring frequently, cook the cabbage for about 15 minutes. The cabbage should melt, in its own juice, as the French say, and do this *without* the addition of any liquid. This is the flavor secret of the dish. Butter a large casserole or roasting dish with a cover. Put half of the cabbage in it. Arrange the partridges on the cabbage and top them with the remaining cabbage. Add the thyme, the bay leaf, and the parsley. Add enough water to come ⅓ way up to the cabbage. Cover tightly and simmer over very low heat for about 1 to 1⅓ hours. Check frequently for moisture; if the dish looks dry and about to scorch, add a little more water. To serve in the best Belgian manner: put the cabbage on a hot, round serving plate. Cut the birds in half lengthwise with poultry shears and put them on the cabbage. Dribble the pan juices over the birds and serve hot, with mashed potatoes.

Note: A richer dish can be made by cooking ½ pound bacon in *one* piece along with the birds and the cabbage. At serving time, the bacon is sliced and arranged around the birds. Blanch the bacon first by pouring boiling water over it and letting it stand for 5 to 10 minutes, or it will be too salty.

PARTRIDGES, WILD DOVES, SNIPE, AND OTHER SMALL GAME BIRDS

Perdreaux, Pigeonneaux, Bécasses, et les Petits Gibiers à Plumes
Serves 6

The Belgians are great hunters, and like the French, they love small—and large—game birds. These are cooked in the usual French ways, and for completeness' sake, though with doubts in my heart as to how many readers will really make up these recipes (unless they are game lovers, and then, they'd know), I give here the two I like best. As for cooking time, it is impossible to say accurately since it depends on the size and the age of the birds. The birds should be trussed.

6 partridges, dressed and trussed	½ cup butter
	6 slices bacon
12 juniper berries, crushed	6 tablespoons cognac
Salt and freshly ground pepper to taste	Toasted bread croutons

Preheat the oven to moderate (350°F.). Put 2 juniper berries into each partridge. Sprinkle the birds inside and out with salt and pepper. Heat the butter in a skillet and brown the birds in it on all sides. Sprinkle with the cognac and flame. Transfer the partridges to a buttered shallow roasting pan. Cover the breast of each bird with 1 slice of bacon. Spoon the skillet drippings over the birds. Roast for about 30 minutes to 1 hour, depending on the kind, the size, and the age of the birds. Baste the birds frequently. Serve the birds on a bed of toasted croutons, surrounded by *Peas with Ham Ardennes Fashion* (page 211) and applesauce or cranberries.

GAME BIRDS COOKED WITH CREAM AND BACON

Gibier à Plumes à l'Ardennaise

This is a method rather than a specific recipe. The bacon makes it *à l'Ardennaise*, since Ardennes cookery relies heavily on the superlative pork products of the region.

If the bird is large, split it into halves; if small, leave it whole. Roll the bird in flour that has been seasoned with salt, pepper, and a dash of nutmeg. Cut blanched, unsliced lean bacon into ½-inch cubes, about ⅓ cup for each bird. Cook the bacon in hot butter until it begins to crisp, but do not let it get too crisp. Remove the bacon with a slotted spoon and reserve. Brown the birds in the butter on all sides. Transfer them to a casserole with a tight lid. Pour in enough *heated* (but not boiled) heavy cream to half cover the birds. Add the bacon. Cover and cook in a preheated moderate oven (350°F.) for 30 minutes to 1 hour, or until the birds are tender. Serve with mashed potatoes and stewed cranberries or applesauce on the side.

JOSETTE'S CHICKEN WITH FOAMY TOPPING

Le Poulet de Josette
Serves 4

The chicken sits under a fluffy blanket of eggs, butter, and cream.

1 3-pound frying chicken, cut into serving pieces
Salt and pepper to taste
1 tablespoon crumbled rosemary
10 tablespoons (1 stick
and 2 tablespoons)
butter
Grated rind and juice of 1 lemon
4 eggs, separated
¼ cup sour cream

Rub the chicken pieces with salt and pepper to taste and the rosemary. Heat 2 tablespoons of the butter in an ovenproof casserole that has a tight cover. Put the remaining butter into a bowl to soften. Brown the chicken pieces in the butter in the casserole. Sprinkle the chicken with the lemon rind and juice. Cook tightly covered on top of the stove for about 20 minutes or until the chicken is about ¾ done. Meantime, beat the softened butter, egg yolks, and sour cream until they are smooth. Beat the egg whites until they are stiff. Fold them gently into the egg mixture. Spoon this mixture evenly over the chicken pieces. Bake the chicken uncovered in a preheated moderate oven (350°F.) for about 15 minutes, or until the topping has set and is golden brown in color. Serve with a piquant vegetable, such as hot cooked green beans or broccoli dressed with lemon and butter.

Note: This dish is rich and does not require an accompanying starch such as noodles, rice, or potatoes. It is also on the bland side, so that if desired, a little wine may be added to the cooking chicken. In this case, let the wine be completely absorbed (by cooking without cover) before adding the topping.

XIV

---◄◆►---

---◄◆►---

Meats

---◄◆►---

BELGIAN BEER COOKERY

Les Plats Aromatisés à la Bière

The Belgians drink even more beer than the Germans, and they have a great many varieties to choose from. They also cook with beer, and beer cookery is encouraged. An excellent volume, *La Cuisine au Pays de Gambrinus*, produced by the distinguished chef Raoul Morleghem, tells of 300 delicious dishes cooked with beer. What this boils down to is that in place of the traditional wine these dishes, of classical French and Belgian ancestry, substitute various beers, which flavor the dish with their specific aroma. Interestingly, the beer does not emerge in the cooked dish as beer, but as a subtle, rather mild mystery ingredient. Thus adventurous palates may develop their own beer cookery with their favorite winey dishes. Unfortunately, in America their scope will be limited since we have so few light and dark beers which really differ from each other. I have found that,

(*164*)

for cooking, the strongest of each kind does best—that is, ale rather than dry beer, and so on—and that beer does well in dishes containing bacon and ham, and it blends extremely well with the cream used to thicken sauces.

PÈRE MARTIN'S BRAISED BEEF

Le Bœuf Braisé du Père Martin
Serves 4 to 6

Marinade:

2 large carrots, chopped
1 large celery stalk, chopped
1 large onion, chopped
2 whole cloves
½ teaspoon ground thyme

2 bay leaves, crumbled
2 cups dark beer
2 tablespoons olive or salad oil
Salt and freshly ground pepper to taste

2 to 3 pounds round of beef, in one piece
1 tablespoon butter

½ cup heavy cream or more

For Garnish:

2 tablespoons butter
¼ pound boiled ham, diced

½ pound mushrooms, cut into quarters
Salt and freshly ground pepper to taste

In a deep dish or a bowl (do not use aluminum) combine the carrots, celery, onion, cloves, thyme, bay leaves, beer, oil, and salt and pepper to taste. Trim excess fat from the meat and add it to the marinade. Cover and refrigerate for 24 hours, turning the meat several times. Remove the meat from the marinade and dry it thoroughly with kitchen paper. Strain the marinade and reserve both the vegetables and the liquid. Heat the butter in a heavy casserole, and over high heat, brown the meat in it on all sides. Transfer the meat to a warm plate and keep it warm. Add the vegetables of the marinade to the casserole, and over high heat, brown them lightly. Return the meat to the casserole and add 1 cup of the marinade liquid, reserving the rest. Cover and simmer either over lowest possible heat for about 2 hours or cook in a preheated moderate oven (350°F.) for the same time or until the meat is tender, but not mushy. (While the meat is cooking, make the garnish.) Turn the meat occasionally and check the moisture; if there is not enough liquid, add a little more beer from the marinade. Transfer the meat to a hot platter and keep it hot. Purée the vegetables and the liquid in the casserole in a food mill or in a blender. Check the seasonings. Return the sauce to the casserole and stir in the cream, or enough cream to make a thickish sauce.

Heat the sauce but do not boil it and keep it warm. Slice the meat, arrange it on a hot platter, and surround it with the garnish. Spoon a little sauce over the meat slices and serve the rest in a gravy boat. Boiled potatoes or buttered noddles go well with this, with a plain green salad.

To make the garnish: Heat the butter in a skillet. Add the ham and the mushrooms. Cook over high heat until the mushrooms are golden brown, but still firm. Season with salt and pepper to taste.

VEAL KIDNEY GAMBRINUS

Rognon de Veau Gambrinus

Serves 1

1 veal kidney
1 tablespoon butter
Belgian or Dijon-type
 mustard
⅓ cup dark beer

1 tablespoon gin,
 preferably Holland gin
⅓ cup heavy cream
Salt and freshly ground
 pepper to taste

Remove the fat and the membrane from the kidney.
Heat the butter in a small skillet. Cook the kidney in it
over medium heat for 2 to 3 minutes, or until it is ¾
done. Transfer the kidney to a hot plate and cut it
crosswise into thin slices, almost through, but so that the
slices are still joined together at the bottom. Spread the
slices with the mustard. Put the kidney together again
and, if necessary, tie it with kitchen string. Return the
kidney to the skillet and add the beer. Finish cooking the
kidney over medium heat for another 2 or 3 minutes.
Remove it to a hot serving dish and keep it hot. Untie it
if it was tied. Add the gin and the cream to the skillet,
and stir, scraping up all the brown bits at the bottom.
Pour the sauce over the kidney and serve hot, with
French-fried potatoes.

SALMIS OF TURKEY FRANS HALS

Salmis de Dinde Frans Hals

This dish comes from the aforementioned *La Cuisine au
Pays de Gambrinus*. I have not made it yet, but since it

sounds rather good, I will translate it, with editorial asides. A very small turkey, weighing 5 to 6 pounds, should be used.

"Cut the turkey into eight pieces and trim them [I would also skin them]. Make a *fumet* [stock] with the neck, gizzard, a few chopped-up veal bones, 1 quart of beef or chicken bouillon, and 1 quart of Louvain beer [dark beer]. Bring to the boiling point, skim, and simmer covered for about 1 hour. Drain the stock. Skim the fat off the stock and blot off all remaining fat blobs with kitchen paper. Reduce to 3 cups.

"Rub the turkey pieces with salt and paprika, dredge them with flour, and sauté them in butter until they are golden on all sides. Put the turkey pieces into a large casserole with the stock (add 3 cups of the stock). (Season with salt and pepper to taste.) Simmer covered until the turkey pieces are ¾ done [about 1 to 1½ hours depending on the size and age of the bird]. Put the meat into another casserole, add [½ pound] mushroom heads sautéed in butter and tiny chipolata sausages [I would omit these] and ½ cup Holland gin. Thicken the stock [with 1 egg yolk beaten with ¼ cup heavy cream], add it to turkey, and finish cooking [covered, over low heat, for about 30 minutes]."

FLEMISH BEER STEW

Carbonnades Flamandes

Serves 4

Flour

*Salt and freshly ground
pepper to taste*

*2 pounds boneless chuck,
cut into 2 x 3-inch slices*

*¼ pound lean bacon,
diced*

2 tablespoons butter

*3 large onions, thinly
sliced*

1 teaspoon sugar

1 tablespoon mild vinegar

1 slice bread

*1 tablespoon Dijon
mustard*

1 bay leaf, crumbled

¼ teaspoon ground thyme

*1 12-ounce bottle of
beer, preferably dark
beer*

Combine the flour, the salt, and the pepper. Dredge the
meat in it, shaking off surplus flour. Cook the bacon in a
heavy skillet until it is transparent. Transfer the bacon
pieces to a casserole and pour off all but 2 tablespoons of
the fat. Add the butter. Brown the onions in the fat and
transfer them to the casserole. Brown the meat on all
sides in the remaining fat and transfer it to the casserole.
Add the sugar and the vinegar. Spread the bread with the
mustard, and add it to the casserole, together with the
bay leaf, thyme, and beer. Simmer covered over low heat
for about ¾ to 1 hour or until the meat is tender. Serve
hot, with plain boiled potatoes and plenty of cold beer.

FLEMISH LEG OF PORK IN BEER

Gestoofd Varkensstuk
Serves 8

6-pound leg of fresh pork,
  skinned and boned,
  or any lean, boneless
  pork
Salt and freshly ground
  pepper to taste
1 large garlic clove,
  halved
3 tablespoons caraway
  seeds

2 tablespoons lard
1 large onion, thinly
  sliced
2 to 3 cups beer or ale
2 teaspoons sugar
1 or 2 slices white bread,
  trimmed of crusts and
  crumbled

Rub the meat with the salt and pepper and garlic on all sides. Pat in the caraway seeds; you may wish to use fewer or more, depending on taste. Heat the lard in a deep casserole or kettle not much larger than the meat. Over high heat, brown the meat in it on all sides. Remove the meat. Add the onion and cook it until it is golden. Remove the onion. Pour off the fat. Return the meat to the casserole and top it with the onion. Add 2 cups of the beer. It should cover the meat completely. Add the sugar and 1 slice of the bread. Cover and simmer over heat for about 3 hours or until the pork is tender. Check the liquid and, if necessary, add the remaining beer. The sauce should be of a medium pancake-batter consistency; if it is too thin, thicken with a little of the remaining bread. Slice the meat before serving and put it on a hot serving dish. Keep hot. Beat the sauce until smooth and drizzle it over the sliced meat. Serve with boiled potatoes or potato dumplings and a cucumber or green salad.

Note: Since American pork is fatter than Belgian pork, it may be necessary to degrease the sauce before taking the meat out of the casserole. Skim off the grease with a spoon. If the meat is taken out first, the fat will get into the sauce.

GROUND MEAT COOKERY

Les Viandes Hachées

Ground meat is extremely popular in Belgium, though it differs from our American ground meat. We favor, or, rather, use ground beef almost exclusively, and make it into hamburgers in the first and meat loaf in the second place. The Belgians like a mixture of beef and lean pork, or lean pork and veal, or a combination of all three. And they like their *fricadelles, boules,* and so on—the Belgian equivalent of hamburgers—to be more solid and flavorful than our own. To this end, they stretch the meat with white bread crumbs (in varying amounts) and egg, and they invariably flavor it with the national spice, ground nutmeg. The meat is sautéed in butter, lard, or bacon fat rather than broiled, and it is much used (more than here) for stuffings.

The following four basic recipes come from *Ons Kookboek,* the cookbook of the Flemish Farmers' Wives' Association, and they show how thrift can become tasty.

Best results are obtained from equal quantities of ground beef and lean pork, or lean pork and veal.

Basic Recipe 1: For each pound of meat, use 1 slice of white bread, 1 egg, salt, pepper, and nutmeg.
Basic Recipe 2: For each pound of meat, use 6 slices of white bread, 3 eggs, salt, pepper, and nutmeg.

Basic Recipe 3: For each pound of meat, use 12 slices of white bread, 6 eggs, salt, pepper, and nutmeg.

Basic Recipe 4: For each ½ pound of meat, use 2 tablespoons fine dry bread crumbs, 2 eggs, salt, pepper, and nutmeg.

Put the meat into a bowl. Cut the crusts off the bread slices and crumble the bread. Add it to the meat, with the eggs and the salt, pepper, and nutmeg. Work the mixture with a spoon or with the hands until it sticks well together.

Note: If ½ pound of ground meat mixture is wanted, use half of the meat and the bread and 1 egg for Basic Recipe 1; 2 eggs for Basic Recipe 2; 3 eggs for Basic Recipe 3; and 2 eggs for Basic Recipe 4.

STUFFED ONIONS

Gevulde Ajuinen
Serves 6

6 *large onions, weighing*
  about ¾ pound each
Boiling *water*
1 *teaspoon salt*
2 *tablespoons butter*
½ *pound ground meat*

mixture (page 171)
2 *tablespoons minced*
  parsley
½ *cup soft white bread*
  crumbs sautéed in 1
  tablespoon butter

Preheat the oven to moderate (350°F.).

Put the onions into a saucepan with 1 inch of boiling water and the salt. Bring to the boiling point, and cook, uncovered, for 5 minutes. Cover and continue cooking for 5 more minutes. Remove the onions and rinse them rapidly under running cold water to cool them. Drain and dry the onions. Remove 5 layers from the center of each onion. Chop it and sauté it in the butter until the onion is soft and golden. Add the meat and cook it, stirring constantly, until it is lightly browned. Stuff the onions with the mixture. Place the onions into a generously buttered baking dish. Sprinkle them with the buttered bread crumbs. Bake the onions for about 45 minutes or until they are tender. Do not overcook them. Serve with any green or vegetable salad.

STUFFED TOMATOES

Gevulde Tomaten
Serves 4 to 6

A beloved family dish.

8 large, firm tomatoes
Salt to taste
Freshly ground pepper to
   taste

½ pound ground meat
   mixture (page 171)
¼ cup minced parsley
Butter

Preheat the oven to moderate (375°F.).

Cut a slice off the bottom of each tomato, opposite the stem end. Reserve the slices. Hollow out the tomatoes with a spoon, taking care not to pierce the shells. Strain the tomato pulp through a coarse sieve and reserve. Salt the inside of the tomatoes lightly and invert them on a rack for 10 minutes, to drain. Season the drained tomatoes with the pepper. Stuff them with the ground meat mixture and sprinkle with the parsley. Place the tomatoes into a baking dish. Add the tomato pulp and enough water to bring the liquid up to ½ inch. Top each tomato with 1 cut-off slice and a little butter.

Bake the tomatoes for about 10 to 15 minutes. Serve from the dish, with boiled potatoes.

OLD-FASHIONED MEAT LOAF

Potée de Boeuf
Serves 6 to 8

¼ cup dried mushrooms
2 pounds ground round
  of beef
½ pound bacon, minced
  or ground
1 large onion, minced
⅓ cup minced parsley

1 slice white bread,
  without crusts
⅓ cup brandy
3 eggs
Salt and freshly ground
  pepper to taste
¼ teaspoon nutmeg

Preheat the oven to moderate (350°F.).

Cover the dried mushrooms with lukewarm water. Let them stand for 15 minutes or until they are soft, then mince them. Combine the mushrooms, the beef, the bacon, the onion, and the parsley and blend them thoroughly. This is best done with clean hands. Soak the bread in the brandy and add the mixture to the first one, together with the eggs, salt and pepper to taste, and the nutmeg. Blend again until the mixture sticks together. Shape it into a loaf and put it into a casserole with a tight-fitting lid. Cover and bake for 2½ to 3 hours. This is good hot or cold.

Note: In old-fashioned country households in the Limbourg province the hot meat loaf was served with boiled potatoes sauced with the pan juices from the meat loaf on the first day, and cold with a mixed salad of potatoes and green beans the next. Excellent.

BIRDS' NESTS

Vogelnestjes
Serves 6

Betty Boulpaep remembers eating them at boarding school.

1 pound ground round
2 eggs
¼ cup fine dry bread crumbs
1 teaspoon salt
¼ teaspoon freshly ground pepper
6 hard-cooked eggs

2 egg whites, beaten until foamy
2 cups fine dry bread crumbs
Deep fat or oil heated to 370°F.
2 cups tomato sauce

Mix the ground round, the eggs, the bread crumbs, and the salt and pepper. Divide the mixture into 6 equal pieces. Flatten each piece and shape it around one hard-cooked egg, enclosing the egg completely. Dip the egg into egg whites and then into crumbs, pressing the crumbs firmly into place. Drop into preheated fat and fry until brown and crusty, about 3 to 5 minutes. Remove with a slotted spoon, drain, and cut into 2 crosswise halves so halves resemble a round bird's nest in which there is ½ an egg. Spoon the heated tomato sauce around the egg halves. Serve hot.

BLIND FINCHES

Blinde Vinken
Serves 6

1 *pound ground lean beef,* ¼ *teaspoon crumbled*
  ground several times   *thyme*
Salt and freshly ground ½ *teaspoon salt*
  pepper to taste ¼ *teaspoon pepper*
6 *veal cutlets, pounded* 1 *cup water*
  until very thin 1 *tablespoon tomato paste*
¼ *cup butter* 2 *tablespoons Madeira*
1 *medium onion, minced* 1 *tablespoon flour mixed*
1 *bay leaf*   *with 2 tablespoons water*

Season the beef with salt and pepper to taste. Roll or pat
it out and cut the meat into 6 equal pieces and put 1
piece on each of the veal cutlets. Roll up the meat. Tie
each roll with kitchen string. Brown the rolls in the hot
butter. Add the onion, bay leaf, thyme, salt and pepper,
and the water. Cover tightly and simmer for 1 hour or
until the veal is tender and the meat is cooked through.
Add a little water from time to time to keep up level of
liquid. Remove the rolls to a hot platter and keep hot.
Stir the tomato paste, the Madeira, and the flour mixture
into pan drippings. Cook over low heat, stirring constantly until the sauce is smooth and thickened. Spoon
the sauce over the veal rolls and serve with boiled potatoes.

BEEF STEW FROM LIMBURG

Bœuf Sauté Limbourgeoise
Serves 4 to 6

¼ *pound lean bacon,*
  diced
1 tablespoon lard
20 small white onions
  (the smaller, the better),
  peeled
2 pounds boneless chuck
  or bottom round, cut
  into 1½-inch cubes

1 large garlic clove,
  chopped
2 tablespoons flour
1 to 2 cups dry red wine
  (a full-bodied wine)
Salt and freshly ground
  pepper to taste
⅓ *cup brandy*

Pour boiling water over the bacon and drain. Combine
the bacon and the lard in a heavy skillet. Cook until the
bacon is limp and transparent. Add the onions and cook,
stirring frequently, until the onions are browned. Transfer the bacon and the onions to a heavy casserole. Add
the meat and the garlic to the fat, and cook over high
heat until it is browned on all sides. Transfer the meat to
the casserole and stir in the flour. Add enough wine to
barely cover the meat and season with salt and pepper to
taste. Bring to the boiling point, lower the heat to very
low, cover the casserole, and simmer for about 1½ hours
or until the meat is tender. Check for moisture; if necessary, add a little more wine. Check the seasoning and stir
in the brandy. Serve with plain boiled potatoes.

Note: Be sure to trim the beef of all fat and gristle.

BUTTER-BROILED STEAK WITH SHALLOTS AND MUSHROOM SAUCE

Entrecôte des Ombiaux
Serves 4

Belgians are very fond of steaks pan-broiled in butter.

2- to 2½-pound steak,
   such as club, Delmonico,
   or sirloin
2 tablespoons butter
2 tablespoons salad oil
Salt and freshly ground
   pepper to taste
3 shallots, minced
3 large mushrooms,
   minced

1 small garlic clove,
   minced
⅔ cup dry white wine
3 tablespoons butter, at
   room temperature
Juice of 1 lemon
2 tablespoons minced
   parsley

Trim the excess fat off the steak and make small cuts all around the steak where there is fat and gristle. This will prevent the meat from curling as it cooks. Heat the butter and the salad oil in a large, heavy skillet until it is almost, but not, smoking. For medium rare, sauté the steak in it on one side for 3 to 4 minutes. Turn the steak and sauté on the other side for 3 to 4 minutes, taking care that the fat in the skillet is not burning, but very hot. Remove the steak to a hot platter, season with salt and pepper, and keep warm. Pour all the fat but 1 tablespoon out of the skillet. Add the shallots, the mushrooms, and the garlic clove. Cook over medium heat, stirring constantly, until the vegetables are soft, but not brown. Stir in the wine. Scrape up the brown bits at the bottom of the skillet. Bring to the boiling point and cook, stirring constantly, until the mixture is reduced by half. Remove from the heat and stir in the softened butter, the lemon juice, and the parsley. Pour the sauce over the steak and serve immediately, with very crisp French-fried potatoes and a watercress salad.

BEEF TONGUE

Rundstong—Warm
Serves 6

Tongue, hot or cold, is a Belgian favorite.

1 smoked beef tongue,
about 3 pounds
4 quarts water
Bouquet garni consisting
of 1 leek, 1 stalk celery,

1 carrot, 1 onion, 6
peppercorns, 1 bay
leaf, and ½ teaspoon
thyme

Cover the tongue with water and let it stand at room temperature for 3 hours. Drain off the water and replace with fresh water. Bring to the boiling point and simmer for 5 minutes. Drain again and replace with fresh boiling water. Add the bouquet garni. Simmer for 2 to 3 hours or until tongue is easily pierced. Drain and peel off skin while the tongue is still warm. Cut the tongue into ¼-inch-thick slices. Serve with your favorite egg sauce, cucumber sauce, mushroom sauce, tomato sauce, or Madeira sauce. If the tongue is sliced ahead of time, reheat slices in bouillon. Garnish slices of tongue with hard-cooked eggs, meatballs, sautéed mushrooms and parsley.

ROAST BEEF

Rosbief
Serves 6

3 *pounds eye round*
2 *tablespoons water*
¼ *cup butter*
1 *onion, quartered*
1 *carrot, sliced*
Salt and freshly ground

pepper to taste
1 *cup boiling water or*
stock
1 *tablespoon potato starch*
mixed with ¼ *cup*
water

Spread half of the butter on the bottom of roasting pan. Put the meat into the pan and spread it with the remaining butter. Roast in a preheated hot oven (400°F.) for 15 minutes. Add 2 tablespoons water and all vegetables to pan. Lower heat to 350°F. and roast for 30 minutes. Sprinkle the meat with salt and pepper. Roast for another 30 minutes. Remove roast to a hot platter and keep warm. Add 1 cup boiling water or stock to the pan drippings. Scrape to loosen all particles. Stir in starch mixture. Stir over low heat until the sauce is smooth and thickened. Cut meat in thin slices across the grain. Spoon sauce over each serving.

Note: Never prick meat during cooking to prevent loosening juices. Roast beef can be prepared in a skillet. Heat butter and brown meat on all sides. Add 2 tablespoons water and vegetables. Cook uncovered over low heat, turning occasionally, for 45 minutes. Season meat with salt and pepper. Cook for another 45 minutes.

MARINATED POT ROAST

Gemarineerde Rosbief
Serves 6

1 3- to 4-pound pot roast
2 cups dry red wine
3 medium onions, sliced
1 stalk celery, sliced
1 leek, sliced
1 carrot, diced
2 parsley sprigs

½ teaspoon crumbled
   thyme
½ lemon, sliced
1 bay leaf
½ cup butter
2 tablespoons flour mixed
   with 2 tablespoons
   water

Combine pot roast, wine, onions, celery, leek, carrot, parsley, thyme, lemon, and bay leaf in a deep bowl, but do not use aluminum. Let stand at room temperature for 1 day. Remove the meat, drain it, and reserve the marinade. Dry the meat. In a Dutch oven, heat the butter, and over high heat brown the meat in it on all sides. Add the marinade, cover tightly, and simmer 2 to 2½ hours or until the meat is easily pierced. When needed, add more water to keep up the level of liquid. Remove the meat to a hot platter and slice. Keep hot. Strain the pan drippings. Stir in the flour mixture and cook over low heat, stirring constantly until the sauce is smooth and thickened. Spoon the sauce over the meat.

LEG OF LAMB À LA GORIS

Gigot à la Façon de Mevrouw Goris
Serves 6 to 8

This recipe comes from a distinguished hostess in Ant-werp who is also an outstanding gardener.

1 leg of lamb	*Cooked green beans,*
1 clove of garlic, mashed	*grilled tomato halves,*
Salt and freshly ground	*sautéed mushrooms or*
pepper to taste	*braised Belgian endives,*
4 large onions, chopped	*potato balls*

Remove all but a very thin layer of fat from the lamb. Rub the meat with the garlic and with the salt and pepper. Put the lamb fat side up into a roasting pan. Roast the lamb until a meat thermometer registers 150°F. for medium rare or 160°F. to 165°F. for well done. A 6-pound leg, with the bone, will take 12 to 15 minutes to the pound for medium rare, and 15 to 20 minutes to the pound for well done. A 4-pound boned and rolled leg will take about 1 ¾ to 2 hours for medium rare, and 2 to 2½ for well done. When the meat is about ¾ done, sprinkle the onions into the pan and continue cooking. Slice the meat, put it on a hot platter, and keep hot. Skim all the excess fat from the drippings and spoon them over the meat. Arrange the vegetables around the meat in neat and attractive heaps.

PORK BRAISED WITH RED CABBAGE

Noix de Porc Choux Rouges
Serves 6

*1 3-pound pork roast,
    boneless*
2 tablespoons cooking fat
*1 tablespoon lard or
    bacon fat*
*1 large onion, thinly
    sliced*
*1 2- to 3-pound red
    cabbage, shredded*

1 cup beef bouillon
*Salt and freshly ground
    pepper to taste*
⅛ teaspoon nutmeg
*⅛ teaspoon ground
    thyme*
2 bay leaves, crumbled
1 teaspoon sugar
⅓ cup water
⅓ cup vinegar

Trim all the excess fat from the pork roast. Brown it in
the cooking fat on all sides in a skillet. Heat the lard in a
large casserole that will hold the pork roast. Cook the
onion in it until it is soft but not brown. Add the cabbage and cook covered over low heat for about 5 minutes, stirring frequently. Add the bouillon, salt, pepper,
nutmeg, thyme, bay leaves, and sugar. Mix well. Put the
pork roast on the cabbage. Pour the fat from the pan in
which the pork was browned. Stir in the water, bringing
up all the brown bits from the bottom. Bring to the
boiling point and pour over the pork. Add the vinegar.
Cover the casserole and simmer over low heat for about
1¾ to 2 hours or until the meat is tender. Do not overcook. Check for moisture during cooking time; if necessary, add a little more bouillon, a few tablespoons at a
time. The dish should be moist, but not soupy. To serve,
carve the pork, put the slices on a hot platter, and sur-

round them with the red cabbage. Mashed potatoes go well with this.

ROAST PORK WITH MUSTARD SAUCE

Rôti de Porc à la Moutarde
Serves 1 for each pound

This dish may be made with a pork loin, leg of pork, or a shoulder. The shoulder should be boned, rolled, and tied. If a loin roast is used, allow about 1 pound for each person since it is very bony. Choose the center cut or the end cut from a loin. The meat should be lean, so trim off any excess fat before cooking it.

*1 4- to 6-pound pork roast
Salt and freshly ground
   pepper to taste
4 tablespoons prepared
   mustard or more to taste
1 tablespoon lard
1 large onion, sliced
1 leek, white and green
   parts, sliced
1 carrot, sliced*

*1 small celery root, sliced,
   or 2 stalks celery, with
   leaves, sliced
½ cup chopped parsley
2 cups consommé or
   water
1 tablespoon flour
2 teaspoons paprika
⅔ cup sour cream
   (optional)*

Preheat the oven to 325°F.

Rub the meat with salt and pepper and coat it with half of the mustard. Heat the lard in a skillet. Sauté the onion, leek, carrot, celery, and parsley in it for 2 to 3 minutes. Using a slotted spoon, transfer the vegetables to a roasting pan. Over high heat, brown the meat in the skillet on all sides. Spread with the remaining mustard. Put the meat on top of the vegetables. Add ½ cup consommé. Roast for about 35 minutes per pound (approximately 3½ hours for a 6-pound roast) or until a meat thermometer inserted in the thickest part of the roast (do not let it touch the bone) registers about 175°F. Baste occasionally with the pan juices. Stir the flour and the paprika into the vegetables and add the remaining consommé. Bring to the boiling point. Taste the seasoning; if necessary, add a little more salt, pepper, and mustard to make a well-flavored gravy. Strain the gravy through a fine sieve or purée in a blender. It should be the consistency of a thin pancake batter. Slice the meat and transfer it to a hot serving platter. Keep it hot. Bring the gravy to the boiling point. Remove it from the heat and stir in the sour cream. Spoon a little of the gravy over the sliced meat and serve the rest in a sauceboat. Serve with mashed potatoes, rice or dumplings.

Note: The thickness of gravies is a matter of personal preference. This, like all gravies, may be thinned with a little more hot bouillon, or thickened with more sour cream.

MARINATED PORK CHOPS

Côtes de Porc St. Hubert

Serves 4

Though the chops may be cooked in butter, it is the lard which gives them their characteristic Belgian flavor.

1 large carrot, sliced
1 large onion, chopped
1 large garlic clove,
chopped
¼ teaspoon ground thyme
2 bay leaves, crumbled
4 whole peppercorns,
crushed
2 cups dry red wine
1 tablespoon olive oil
4 pork chops, about 1¼-
inch thick, center or
rib loin

Salt and freshly ground
pepper to taste
2 tablespoons lard
Beurre manié *made with*
½ tablespoon butter
and ½ tablespoon flour
(optional)
1 tablespoon red currant
jelly
2 teaspoons Dijon-type
mustard
Juice of ½ lemon

Combine the carrot, onion, garlic, thyme, bay leaves, peppercorns, wine, and olive oil in a saucepan. Bring to the boiling point and simmer covered for 5 minutes. Cool completely. Trim all but the thinnest layer of fat from the pork chops and level the corners of the backbone so that the chops will lie flat. Season the chops lightly with salt and pepper. Put the chops into a deep container (do not use aluminum) and pour the marinade over them. Cover the container and refrigerate the chops for at least one day, turning them over once. When ready to cook the chops, take them out of the marinade and dry them on kitchen toweling. Reserve the marinade. Heat the lard in a deep skillet. Over high heat, brown the chops on each side for about 2 minutes. Lower the heat and pour off all the fat from the pan. Pour the marinade over the chops. Cover the skillet. Cook over low heat for about 25 to 30 minutes. Turn the chops over twice and baste them at intervals. When they are done, remove them to a hot platter and keep them hot. Cook down the pan juices to about 1¼ cup. Skim the excess fat from the sauce. Stir in the *beurre manié*, the red currant jelly, the mustard, and the lemon. Bring to the boiling point and remove at once from the heat. Strain the sauce through a fine strainer over the pork chops. Serve immediately, with mashed or gratin potatoes.

Note: The *beurre manié* will thicken the sauce. People who like thinner sauces can leave it out.

MARINATED PORK

Filet de Porc a l'Escavèche
Serves 4 to 6

A very good dish, hot or cold. Besides, pork is always with us.

1 4-pound loin of pork, center cut or rib cut, boned and rolled, to make about 3 lbs. boneless meat
1 teaspoon salt
½ teaspoon freshly ground pepper
1 teaspoon dried thyme
1 teaspoon dried tarragon
2 bay leaves, crumbled
8 juniper berries, crushed
1 large garlic clove, mashed
2 cups dry white wine
1 cup white vinegar
¼ cup olive oil

1 large carrot, chopped fine
2 celery stalks, chopped fine
3 green onions, chopped fine
2 large tomatoes, peeled and chopped
3 garlic cloves, mashed
Salt and freshly ground pepper to taste
2 sprigs fresh tarragon or 1 tablespoon dried tarragon
2 tablespoons olive oil
½ cup minced parsley
Lemon wedges

Cut all fat off the pork except for a ⅛-inch layer. Combine the salt, pepper, thyme, tarragon, bay leaves, juniper berries, and garlic clove in a small bowl and mix them thoroughly. Rub the mixture into the pork on all sides. Put the meat into a deep bowl or casserole, but do not use an aluminum one which would disfigure the meat. Cover and refrigerate for 2 hours. Combine the wine and vinegar and pour the mixture over the meat. Marinate for at least 4 hours or overnight. Turn and baste the pork occasionally so that the meat will be marinated on all sides. Just before cooking time, take out the pork and dry it thoroughly. Strain and reserve the marinade. Heat the oil in a saucepan and add the carrot, celery, and green onions. Cook over medium heat until the vegetables are tender, but not brown. Pour off any excess oil. Add the tomatoes and the garlic. Season with salt and pepper and add the tarragon. Cover and cook the mixture over low heat for 10 minutes. Skim off any fat that may have risen to the surface and add 1 cup of the reserved marinade and put aside. In a large casserole, heat the 2 tablespoons oil, and over high heat brown the pork in it on all sides, for about 7 to 10 minutes. Turn the pork so that the fattiest side is up and lower the heat to simmering. Cover the casserole and cook for about 10 minutes, taking care the meat does not scorch. Pour off any excess fat and add the vegetable mixture, spooning it over the meat. Simmer covered for about 1½ hours or until the meat is tender. A 3-pound boned and rolled loin of pork cooks in about 1¾ to 2 hours. Baste the meat frequently and turn it once. If there is not enough cooking liquid, add a little more of the reserved marinade, a tablespoon at a time. Put the cooked meat into a deep serving dish. Degrease the sauce in which it has cooked, and pour it over the pork. Sprinkle with the parsley and serve hot or cold, with lemon wedges as a garnish. *Flemish Potatoes* (page 214) go well with the hot meal, and a *Salade Liégeoise* (page 107) would be nice with the cold pork.

PORK ROASTED WITH APPLES

Rôti de Porc aux Pommes
Serves 4 to 6

1 4-pound loin of pork, center cut or rib cut, boned and rolled to make about 3 pounds boneless meat
Salt to taste

2 tablespoons butter, at room temperature
1 cup water
6 large tart apples, peeled, cored, and quartered
Salt and freshly ground pepper to taste

Preheat the oven to hot (425°F.).

Cut all fat off the pork except for a ⅛-inch layer. Rub the salt into all the surface of the meat. Rub the butter only into the meat proper and not into the fat. Put the pork into the oven. Cook for about 10 minutes. If the fat from the pork begins to scorch, add ½ cup of the water. Lower the oven heat to low (325°F.). If no water was added, now pour ½ cup into pan. If water has been added, pour in another ¼ cup. Arrange the apple quarters around the pork and season them with salt and pepper. Cook for about 1½ hours or until the meat is tender. A 3-pound boned and rolled loin of pork cooks in about 1¾ to 2 hours. Slice the pork, place the slices on a hot platter, and surround them with the apples which will have cooked down.

PORK OR VEAL ROAST

Varkenbraad; Kalfbraad
Serves 6

3 pounds loin of pork or
a 3-pound veal roast
(shoulder or leg)
¼ cup butter (for veal
only)

Salt and freshly ground
pepper to taste
Thyme
1 cup boiling water
½ cup heavy cream
2 teaspoons potato starch

Place the pork or veal on a rack in a shallow pan. If roasting veal spread it with butter. Roast in a preheated moderate oven (350°F.) 45 minutes for veal and 1 hour for pork. Remove the meat from oven and sprinkle it with salt, pepper, and thyme. Replace it in the oven and roast the veal another 45 minutes and pork for another hour. Remove the roast to a hot platter and keep warm. Stir 1 cup boiling water into the pan drippings. Scrape to loosen all particles. Mix the cream and potato starch and stir into the roasting pan. Cook over low heat, stirring constantly, until the sauce thickens slightly. Cut meat into slices and spoon the hot sauce over it.

SWEETBREADS

Kalfszwezeriken
Serves 4 to 6

2 pairs sweetbreads
Water
2 teaspoons salt
½ cup butter
½ pound mushrooms,
   sliced
¼ cup flour

1 cup chicken broth
1 cup (½ pint) light
   cream
1 egg yolk
Salt and freshly ground
   pepper to taste

Cover the sweetbreads with cold water. Let stand at room temperature for 2 hours, changing the water 2 times. Drain, add cold water to cover, and the salt. Bring to the boiling point, lower the heat, and simmer for 15 to 20 minutes, or until sweetbreads are firm and white throughout. Drain and rinse with cold water. Remove the membranes and cut the sweetbreads into large pieces. Heat the butter and sauté mushrooms in it until they are wilted and pale golden. Stir in the flour. Gradually stir in the chicken broth. Beat the light cream and egg yolk and stir the mixture into the sauce. Cook over low heat, stirring constantly until the sauce is smooth and thickened. Season with salt and pepper. Fold in the sweetbreads and reheat but do not boil. Spoon onto a warmed platter. Garnish with parsley.

VEAL KIDNEYS LIÉGEOISE

Rognons de Veau a la Liégeoise
Serves 2 to 4

*4 veal kidneys, trimmed
and split into halves
4 tablespoons butter
1 tablespoon juniper
berries, crushed
1 bay leaf, crumbled*

*1 tablespoon Holland-
type gin or brandy
1 tablespoon water
Salt and freshly ground
pepper to taste
Butter-fried croutons*

Preheat the oven to 400°F. On top of the stove, heat the
butter in a shallow baking dish that is presentable enough
to go to the table. Brown the kidneys in it on all sides.
Transfer the dish to the oven. Cook the kidneys for 10 to
15 minutes, depending on size, but do not overcook them
or they will be tough. Turn the kidneys frequently. Add
the juniper berries, bay leaf, gin, water, and season with
salt and pepper to taste. Heat through for about 3 minutes and sprinkle with the croutons before serving.

Note: To trim the veal kidneys, cut off all the fat and
white membrane.

VEAL ROAST ORLOFF

Kalfsgebraad Orloff
Serves 6 to 8

*3 pounds veal roast from
the shoulder or leg
Salt and freshly ground
pepper to taste
¼ cup butter
7 slices smoked ham or
tongue*

*7 slices Swiss cheese
1 cup thick cheese sauce
⅓ cup fine dry bread
crumbs
2 tablespoons butter*

Sprinkle the roast with salt and pepper and spread it with the butter. Roast on a rack in a shallow pan in a pre-heated moderate oven (350°F.) for 1½ hours or until tender. Cut the meat into 8 slices. Place 1 ham slice and 1 cheese slice between each of the veal slices. Fasten together with 2 skewers. Put the roast into a shallow pan. Spoon cheese sauce over slices. Sprinkle with the crumbs and dot with the 2 tablespoons butter. Bake in a pre-heated moderate oven (350°F.) for 30 minutes or until heated through. Garnish with sautéed onions, potato balls, and parsley.

VEAL CUTLETS WITH MUSHROOMS

Kalfskoteletten met Champignons
Serves 4 to 6

6 veal cutlets or
* scalloppini*
Salt and freshly ground
* pepper to taste*
¼ cup butter
1 can (6 ounces) sliced

* mushrooms*
1 beef bouillon cube
Water
2 teaspoons potato starch
* or cornstarch*

Sprinkle veal with salt and pepper. Brown veal slowly in butter. Put on a hot platter and keep veal warm in a 300°F. oven. Drain the mushrooms and reserve juice. Add the bouillon cube and enough water to make 1 cup. Stir potato starch or cornstarch into the pan drippings. Gradually stir in the liquid. Cook over low heat, stirring constantly, until the sauce is smooth and thickened. Fold in the mushrooms and reheat. Serve the veal cutlets with mushrooms spooned over them.

VEAL SAUTÉ

Kalfssautés
Serves 4 to 6

6 boneless veal cutlets
Salt and freshly ground
 pepper to taste
2 egg whites, beaten until
 foamy

2 cups fine dry bread
 crumbs
½ cup butter
¼ cup heavy cream

Sprinkle the veal with salt and pepper on both sides. Dip the veal into egg whites. Dip the veal into the bread crumbs, pressing them firmly in place. Heat the butter and fry the veal slowly until it is browned on both sides. It takes 15 minutes to fry meat properly. Remove the meat to a hot platter and keep warm. Stir the cream into the pan drippings. Scrape to loosen all particles. Spoon the sauce over veal.

Boneless pork cutlets may be prepared in the same way. However the meat must be fried slowly, allowing 20 minutes for pork to be cooked thoroughly.

MARINATED HARE

Gemarineerde Haas
Serves 6

Belgian hares are lovely beasts which combine nobility with cuddlesomeness. The best European artists have drawn and painted them with loving care for their beauty and, no doubt, hope for the delightful dishes they can be turned into. They are highly prized in Belgium as in all of Europe. Incidentally, European hares are not rabbits; they are all dark meat while American domestic hares are white meat. If at all possible, save the blood for the sauce. It is an excellent thickener and flavor maker.

1 hare, fresh or frozen,
    thawed; reserve the
    heart and the liver

Marinade:
2 cups dry red wine
½ cup wine vinegar
Yellow peel of 1 lemon
1 large onion, chopped
1 large carrot, chopped

1 cup sliced celery
1 bay leaf
1 teaspoon dried thyme
6 peppercorns
½ teaspoon ground
    nutmeg

To cook and sauce the
    hare:
6 tablespoons butter
⅓ cup minced bacon or
    blanched salt pork
1 large onion, minced
½ pound mushrooms,
    sliced
Salt and freshly ground
    pepper to taste
½ teaspoon dried thyme

1 bay leaf
Hare's blood, heart, and
    liver
¼ cup heavy cream
¼ cup cognac
½ square (½ ounce)
    unsweetened chocolate
1 tablespoon cornstarch
    or potato starch
2 tablespoons water

Cut the hare (or have it cut) into 6 pieces: front legs with halved chest, hind legs and halved saddle. Refrigerate the blood, heart, and liver. Combine all the marinade ingredients in a large glass, china, enamel, or stainless steel bowl, but do not use aluminum. Mix well and add the hare pieces. Cover and refrigerate for from 1 to 3 days, depending on the age of the hare. Turn the pieces once a day. Remove the hare from the marinade and reserve the marinade. Dry the meat thoroughly. In a large skillet, heat the butter and cook the bacon in it until it is transparent. Do not brown it. Over high heat, brown the hare pieces in the mixture until they are golden brown. Transfer them to a large casserole or kettle. Brown the onion and the mushrooms in the same skillet. With a slotted spoon, take them out of the fat and add them to the hare. Season with salt and pepper to taste. Add the thyme and bay leaf. Add 1 cup of the marinade. Simmer covered over low heat for 2 to 2½ hours or until tender; cooking time depends on the age of the hare. Check frequently for moisture and add more marinade as it is needed to keep the hare from drying out. It should not cook in a lot of liquid, but just enough to keep it moist. Mince the hare's heart and liver. Combine them with the blood (if any) and ½ cup of the marinade. Simmer covered for 5 to 10 minutes. While the mixture is cooking, transfer the hare to a hot platter and keep it hot. Skim off the fat from the liquid in which it cooked. Remove the blood, liver and heart mixture from the heat and strain into the hare liquid. Stir in the heavy cream, the cognac, and then add the chocolate. Blend the cornstarch with the water to a smooth paste and stir it into the sauce. Return to low heat and cook, stirring constantly, until the sauce is smooth and thickened. Check the seasonings and spoon the sauce over the hare. Serve with applesauce and boiled potatoes.

Note: It is impossible to be scientifically accurate about the amount of the sauce's ingredients, since this depends on the size of the hare, the amount of liquid it needed cooking, and so on. However, the sauce should be of the usual consistency, not too thick and not thin. I would think that anybody ambitious enough to cook hare would know how to make a sauce of the proper consistency.

RABBIT, FLEMISH STYLE

Konijn op zijn Vlaams
Serves 6

An excellent supper dish, with a good dark bread and sweet butter and applesauce or stewed prunes on the side.

4 ounces salt pork
½ cup butter
3 large onions, thinly sliced
1 rabbit, fresh or frozen, thawed and cut into pieces (reserve liver)
3 bay leaves
1½ cups dry red wine

2 tablespoons wine vinegar
1 cup water
2 teaspoons sugar
Salt and freshly ground pepper to taste
2 tablespoons cornstarch or potato starch
¼ cup water

Pour boiling water over the salt pork and let it stand for 3 minutes. Drain and cube the salt pork. In a skillet, heat ¼ cup of butter and cook the salt pork in it until it is crisp. Add the onions and cook them until they are soft and golden. In a large casserole or kettle, heat the remaining butter and over high heat cook the rabbit pieces in it until they are golden brown on all sides. Add the salt pork, the onions, and their pan juices to the rabbit. Add the bay leaves, wine, vinegar, water, and sugar. Season with salt and pepper to taste. Cover tightly and simmer for 1½ to 2 hours, or until tender; cooking time depends on the age of the rabbit. Transfer the rabbit pieces to a hot platter and keep hot. Skim the excess fat off the pan liquid and remove the bay leaves. Blend the cornstarch with the water to a smooth paste. Stir it into the pan liquid. Cook over low heat, stirring frequently, until thickened. Spoon the sauce over the rabbit pieces and serve.

SAUCE FOR GAME

Sauce pour Gibier
About 2 cups

1 cup red currant jelly
1 cup dry red wine
⅛ teaspoon ground ginger
⅛ teaspoon ground cloves
1 tablespoon fresh lemon
  juice

1 or 2 tablespoons pan
  gravy, strained
  (optional)
1 tablespoon butter
2 teaspoons flour
1 tablespoon cognac

Melt the red currant jelly in a saucepan over low heat. Stir in the wine, ginger, cloves, and lemon juice. Simmer covered for 5 to 10 minutes. If there is any pan gravy from the game, stir in 1 or 2 tablespoons. Knead together the butter and the flour and stir it in small pieces into the sauce. Continue simmering, stirring frequently, for about 3 minutes. Remove from the heat and stir in the cognac. Serve in a sauceboat.

XV

Vegetables

FLEMISH ASPARAGUS

Asperges à la Flamande
Serves 4

Belgian asparagus is snow white, fat and juicy. Imported, canned, or bottled white asparagus is available in this country, and it may be used instead of fresh asparagus, heated gently in its own juice, and then drained.

2 pounds asparagus,
  trimmed, peeled, and
  cooked
4 hard-cooked eggs
1 cup butter, melted
Salt and freshly ground
  pepper to taste

1 tablespoon fresh lemon
  juice or ⅛ teaspoon
  ground nutmeg
2 tablespoons minced
  parsley

Drain the asparagus thoroughly on a kitchen towel. Line a serving platter with a linen napkin and place the asparagus on it; this will absorb any remaining moisture.

Crush the eggs in a small bowl and stir in the remaining ingredients. Serve in a sauceboat with the asparagus.

Or, family style, let each diner help himself to 1 hard-cooked egg and mash it on his own plate. Combine the butter, salt, pepper, and lemon juice in a sauceboat and pass around, for each diner to sprinkle on his mashed egg and asparagus.

GREEN BEANS VELOUTÉ

Haricots Verts au Velouté
Serves 3 to 4

The sauce of this recipe is equally good for cooked hot cauliflower, broccoli, Belgian endives, and Brussels sprouts.

1½ pounds green beans
1 tablespoon butter
1 tablespoon flour
1½ cups water or
*   chicken bouillon*
2 egg yolks
Juice of 1 lemon

¼ cup heavy cream or 1
*   tablespoon butter, at*
*   room temperature*
Salt and freshly ground
*   pepper to taste*
⅓ cup minced parsley

Cook the green beans in plenty of boiling salted water until they are barely tender and drain them. While they are cooking, make the sauce. In a saucepan large enough to hold the cooked beans, melt the butter. Stir in the flour and cook, stirring constantly, for about 1 minute. Stir in the water. Cook covered over lowest possible heat, stirring frequently, for about 5 minutes. In a bowl, beat the egg yolks with the lemon juice. Carefully beat in the cream or the butter. Stir about ¼ cup of the hot sauce into the egg-yolk mixture. Stir the egg-yolk mixture into the remaining sauce. Add the beans and cook, stirring constantly, for about 2 to 3 minutes or until the beans are heated through. Keep the heat as low as possible, using an asbestos plate over the heat if necessary, or the sauce will curdle. Remove from the heat and season lightly with salt and pepper. Turn into a serving dish and sprinkle with parsley and serve with roast meats.

CREAMED CABBAGE

Chou à la Crème
Serves 4

This is a lighter dish than our American creamed cabbage.

1 medium cabbage, coarsely shredded	*Salt and freshly ground pepper to taste*
4 tablespoons butter	*Nutmeg to taste*
1 cup milk or light cream	

Blanch the cabbage—that is, cook it in boiling salted water for about 2 to 3 minutes. Drain the cabbage and press out excess moisture. Put the cabbage into a saucepan. Add the butter, the milk, the salt, pepper, and nutmeg to taste. Simmer covered over low heat, stirring frequently, for about 10 minutes or until the cabbage is tender but not overcooked.

RED CABBAGE WITH APPLES

Choux Rouge aux Pommes
6 servings

A national favorite and a dish that can be prepared ahead of time and reheated when needed.

2 *tablespoons lard or*
   bacon fat
6 *slices bacon, minced*
2 *large onions, thinly*
   sliced
1 *firm head red cabbage,*
   thinly sliced (about 8
   to 10 cups)

4 *tart cooking apples,*
   peeled, cored, and sliced
1 *tablespoon sugar*
¼ *cup water*
Salt and freshly ground
   pepper to taste
¼ *teaspoon ground*
   nutmeg

Combine the lard, minced bacon, and the onions in a heavy casserole. Over low heat, and stirring frequently, cook the mixture until the onions are soft. Do not brown them. Add the cabbage. Cover and lower the heat. Cook over low heat, *without* stirring, for 15 minutes. Shake the casserole occasionally and check if the cabbage shows signs of scorching. If this is the case, add a little water. Add the apples, sugar, water, salt, pepper, and nutmeg. Stir to blend. Simmer covered over low heat for 1½ hours. Serve with any pork dish or roast duck or pheasant.

Note: The long, slow cooking is essential to the flavor of the dish.

CARROTS COOKED WITH BACON

Carottes au Lard
Serves 4

A welcome change, but since this dish is more substantial than the usual way of cooking carrots, I serve it as the sole side dish to roast pork or veal, rather than with potatoes.

12 *medium carrots*
Boiling water
6 *slices bacon, diced*
1 *tablespoon butter*
1 *large onion, minced*
1 *tablespoon flour*
1 *cup water*

Salt and freshly ground
  pepper to taste
Nutmeg to taste
1 *teaspoon sugar*
2 *tablespoons minced*
  parsley

Cut the carrots into 1¼-inch slices, and cut these slices into sticks. Pour boiling water over the bacon and drain. Cook the bacon in the butter until it is limp. Add the onion and cook until the onion is soft and just turning golden. Stir in the flour and the water. Season with salt, pepper, and nutmeg to taste and stir in the sugar. Add the carrots. Cook covered over low heat, stirring frequently, for about 20 minutes or until the carrots are just tender. Sprinkle the parsley over the carrots before serving.

FLEMISH CARROTS

Carottes à la Flamande
Serves 4 to 6

8 *medium carrots, cut*
  into small sticks
½ *cup water*
½ *cup butter*
Salt and freshly ground
  pepper to taste
1 *teaspoon sugar*

2 *egg yolks*
½ *to* ⅔ *cup heavy cream*
2 *tablespoons melted*
  butter
2 *tablespoons lemon juice*
2 *tablespoons minced*
  parsley

Pour boiling water over the carrots and cook them for 3 minutes. Drain the carrots. Put them into a buttered

(203)

casserole. Add the water, butter, salt, pepper, and sugar. Bring to the boiling point and reduce heat to low. Cook covered for 15 minutes or until the carrots are tender but not overcooked; the cooking time depends on their age. Shake the casserole every 3 or 4 minutes to prevent sticking, and, if necessary, add a little more water. But if the carrots are soupy, cook them uncovered to let the excess liquid evaporate. Beat together the egg yolks, the cream, the melted butter, and the lemon juice. Add the sauce to the carrots and heat through but do not boil. Sprinkle with the parsley and serve immediately.

BELGIAN ENDIVES

Chicons—Witloof

This splendid white vegetable, one of the most appetizing ones in the whole vegetable world, is as good hot and cooked as in the better-known salads. It can be served as a perfect accompaniment to meats, especially veal, or in entrees that stand on their own feet.

The best Belgian endives have firm white heads. They must not be exposed to daylight, but kept covered with kitchen paper. In the refrigerator, they must not be exposed to very cold temperatures, but kept in a covered vegetable crisper. Before using, the outer leaves, which may be brown at the edges, should be thrown away and the stem end trimmed. If the slightly bitter taste of Belgian endives is found painful (I personally adore it), do the following. Using a small, sharp, and pointed knife, cut off a very thin slice from the stem end of each head. Then make a small incision into the core of the Belgian endive and scoop it out to the depth of ⅓ to ¼ inch. Belgian endives must be washed quickly and never left to soak in water or they'll get soggy. Shake off the excess water from the leaves and dry them before using.

When Belgian endives are used for cooking, choose firm heads of equal size, so that they will cook in the same time. Lay them side by side, in one or two layers in a saucepan that will just hold them, so that they won't rattle around when they are cooking and have their leaves come undone like an untidy coiffure. The saucepan should also have a tight cover. Cook the vegetable in very little water since it is watery enough on its own. And never, never cook Belgian endives (or other vegetables, for that matter) in an iron saucepan or skillet because they'll darken. A little lemon juice in the cooking water will keep the Belgian endives even whiter and prettier.

Best of all, there are only 47 calories to the pound of Belgian endives.

BELGIAN ENDIVES AU GRATIN

Chicons Gratinés
Serves 4

8 *medium or large firm Belgian endives*	½ *cup grated Swiss cheese*
3 *tablespoons butter*	*Salt and cayenne pepper to taste*
2 *tablespoons flour*	
1½ *cups milk*	½ *cup fine dry bread crumbs*
½ *cup light or heavy cream*	2 *tablespoons melted butter*

Preheat the oven to moderate (375°F.).

Wash and dry the endives and place them in the bottom of a buttered 2-quart casserole. Heat the butter in a saucepan, stir in the flour, and cook, stirring constantly, for 2 minutes. Stir in the milk and the cream and continue cooking, stirring all the time, until the sauce is smooth and thickened. Remove the sauce from the heat and stir in the cheese, season with salt and cayenne pepper to taste. Pour the sauce over the Belgian endives. Sprinkle with the bread crumbs and drizzle the melted butter over the bread crumbs. Bake for about 25 to 30 minutes or until the crumbs are golden and the sauce bubbly.

Note: A complete entree may be prepared with this dish by adding 1 to 1½ cups cooked chopped crabmeat or cooked, shelled, and chopped shrimps to the sauce.

BRAISED BELGIAN ENDIVES

Chicons Braisés
Serves 4

3 tablespoons butter	⅓ cup water
1 pound Belgian endives, trimmed and washed	1 tablespoon fresh lemon juice
¼ teaspoon salt	

Butter a shallow casserole or baking dish with 1 tablespoon of the butter. Lay the endives in it, in a single or a double layer, depending on the size of the dish. Add the salt, the water, and the lemon juice and dot with the remaining butter. Cover tightly and cook over low heat for about 10 minutes. Uncover and cook for about 5 to 10 minutes longer, or until the Belgian endives are tender but not mushy, and the pan juices are reduced to 2 or 3 tablespoons.

Note: For a golden effect, drizzle 2 tablespoons melted butter over the braised endives and put them briefly under the broiler to let them get a lovely golden brown color.

BELGIAN ENDIVES AND HAM AU GRATIN

Chicons au Jambon Gratinés
Serves 4

8 large Belgian endives	½ cup grated Swiss cheese
1 tablespoon lemon juice	1 egg yolk
1 teaspoon salt	Salt and freshly ground
Water	pepper to taste
2 tablespoons butter	8 slices boiled ham
2 tablespoons flour	2 tablespoons grated
1¼ cups milk	Parmesan cheese

Trim the endives at the stalk and remove any brown-edged leaves. Wash and dry them. Put the endives into a saucepan with the lemon juice, salt, and just enough water to cover. Simmer covered for about 10 to 15 minutes, or until the endives are just tender. Drain the vegetables. Meanwhile, heat the butter in a saucepan and stir the flour into it. Cook for about 2 minutes, stirring constantly. Add the milk. Cook, stirring all the time, until the sauce is thick and smooth. Add the Swiss cheese and cook until the cheese is melted. Remove from the heat and beat in the egg yolk. Season with salt and pepper to taste. Wrap the endives in the ham slices and place them in a shallow buttered baking dish. Pour the cheese sauce over the vegetables and sprinkle with the Parmesan cheese. Bake in a preheated moderate oven (375°F.) for about 20 minutes or until the top is browned and bubbly, or brown under a broiler.

Note: This dish can be made ahead of time, refrigerated, and browned in the oven just before serving, since the broiler would not heat it through properly before browning the top. Make sure that the vegetables are well drained and the *béchamel* thick. Do not leave the dish too long in the oven or you will wind up with a watery sauce.

BRAISED ESCAROLE

Endives Braisées
Serves 4

This dish may also be made with chicory or Romaine lettuce. It is an excellent, year-round cooked vegetable dish which deserves to be far better known in the United States, where we tend to use these greens for salads only.

2 *large heads escarole*
1 *medium onion, minced*
2 *tablespoons butter*
Salt *and freshly ground*
    pepper to taste
Beurre Manié *made with 2*

tablespoons butter and
2 *tablespoons flour*
2 *to 3 tablespoons milk*
    (*optional*)
Small *croutons fried in*
butter

Remove any wilted or bruised outer leaves from the escarole. Shred it coarsely. Wash the greens and dry them. In a large saucepan, cook the onion in the butter until it is soft, but not brown. Add the lettuce and season it with salt and pepper to taste. Cook covered over low heat, stirring frequently, for about 10 minutes, or until the lettuce is tender, but do not overcook it. Stir the *beurre manié* into it, a teaspoonful at a time. If the sauce is too thick, add the milk, a little at a time, until the right consistency is achieved. Turn the escarole into a serving dish and sprinkle it with the croutons. Serve with roast meats, roast duck, or roast chicken.

CREAMED HOPS

Les Jets de Houblon

Countries that make and drink a lot of beer also have a lot of hops. The young shoots make a most delicious and delicate vegetable, during three weeks only in May. I don't think hop shoots are sold commercially in this country, but perhaps they are available where hops are grown. This is a simple way of preparing them. Asparagus recipes apply to hop shoots. Put the hop shoots into a casserole, add enough boiling salted water to cover, and the juice of 1 lemon. Cook for a few minutes or just until tender. Drain the hops. Serve them with a sauce made with a little heavy cream heated together with butter (1 tablespoon butter for each ½ cup heavy cream) and seasoned with salt and freshly ground pepper. Spoon the hops and their sauce into a deep serving dish and top them with poached eggs. This is a very popular first course.

MUSHROOM CASSEROLE

Fricassée de Champignons
Serves 3 to 4

1 pound small mushrooms, whole
4 to 6 slices lean bacon, diced
4 big shallots, minced, or 1 medium onion, minced
1 tablespoon flour
1 cup dry white wine
Salt and freshly ground pepper to taste
⅛ teaspoon ground nutmeg
Herb butter made by kneading together 1 tablespoon softened butter, 1 tablespoon minced parsley, and (optional) ½ tablespoon fresh or dry crumbled tarragon

Trim and wash the mushrooms quickly under running cold water and drain. Cook the bacon in a heavy casserole until it is soft but not crisp. Add the shallots and cook, stirring constantly, until they are tender but not browned. Stir in the flour and add the wine, salt and pepper to taste, and the nutmeg. Bring to the boiling point and add the mushrooms. Cook covered for 5 minutes or until the mushrooms are just tender; cooking time depends on their size. Check for the liquid; if there is too large an amount of pan liquid, cook uncovered, over higher heat, to reduce. The dish should have a reasonable amount of sauce, but not be soupy. Stir in the herb butter just before serving. Serve very hot, with roast meats or fowl.

DEEP-FRIED PARSLEY

Persil Frit

This excellent Belgian accompaniment to practically every kind of dish deserves to be better known in America.

Wash the parsley. Shake it dry and dry it extremely thoroughly on paper towels. Make sure no water remains on the parsley or the fat in which it will be fried will spatter. Heat the frying fat or oil to 375°F. on the frying thermometer. Put the parsley into a frying basket or drop it by clusters directly into the hot fat. Fry only until the parsley surfaces and has become crisp. This will take 10 to 15 seconds. Do not overfry or the color will change. Drain on paper towels and serve immediately.

PEAS WITH HAM ARDENNES FASHION

Petits Pois à l'Ardennaise
Serves 4

¼ pound smoked ham or
Canadian bacon or
prosciutto ham
1 tablespoon butter
1 medium onion, thinly
sliced
1 large Boston lettuce,
shredded
½ cup water
3 pounds fresh peas,
shelled (about 3 cups)
1 tablespoon flour
Salt and freshly ground
pepper to taste
Beurre manié made with 1
tablespoon butter, ½
tablespoon flour, and 1
tablespoon minced
parsley

Cut the ham into thin julienne strips. Put the ham, the butter, the onion, and the lettuce into a casserole. Cook over low heat, stirring frequently, for about 5 minutes. Add the water and cook for 5 minutes longer. Add the peas, mix well, and stir in the flour. Season with salt and pepper to taste. Simmer covered for about 10 minutes or until the peas are tender, but do not overcook them. Stir frequently; if the dish is soupy, cook uncovered to let the excess liquid evaporate. Remove from the heat and stir in the *beurre manié*.

Note: If the peas are really good young ones, this dish would be nice to eat as a separate course, with thinly sliced brown bread and butter.

FRENCH-FRIED POTATOES

Frites
Serves 6

The Belgians prefer the twice-fried method for French-fried potatoes, and so do I. It makes for a crisper, well-cooked potato, and it has the advantage that you can do the frying at any time that is convenient, keeping the re-frying for serving time. The Belgian frites are smaller than our standard French-fries and I also think this an advantage. Use old potatoes—new ones will not deep-fry properly. Use a frying basket or a strainer to fry the potatoes in.

6 large old potatoes   *Salt*   *Fat for deep-frying*

Peel the potatoes. Cut them lengthwise into strips 2 inches by ¼ inch, or smaller and thinner. Soak the potatoes for about 30 minutes in slightly salted ice water. Drain thoroughly between kitchen paper first and then in kitchen towels. If the potatoes are not well drained, they will spatter in the fat. Divide the potatoes into several equal portions of about 1 cup each. Do not fry too many at one time. Heat the fat to 350°F. Fry the potatoes in this fat until they are tender but not at all browned, about 2 to 3 minutes. The potatoes should be rather limp. Remove the potatoes and drain them in kitchen paper. Cool them thoroughly before the second frying. Keep in a cool spot, but not in the refrigerator. At serving time, heat the fat to 390°F. Fry the potatoes in small batches until they are golden brown and crisp.

Drain on absorbent paper, sprinkle with salt, and serve immediately, in a napkin-lined basket.

Note: Never cover French-fried potatoes or they will go flabby.

POTATO CROQUETTES

Croquettes de Pommes de Terre
Serves 6

They are festive and not nearly as much trouble to make as people think. Use old potatoes—new ones don't hold together well.

2 pounds old potatoes	⅛ teaspoon ground
4 tablespoons butter	nutmeg
3 egg yolks	Melted butter
1 egg	2 egg whites
Salt and freshly ground	Fine dry bread crumbs
pepper to taste	

Peel the potatoes and cut them into pieces. Cook in boiling salt water to cover until they are tender, but not mushy. Drain the potatoes and push them through a fine sieve or rice them with a potato ricer. Return the purée to the saucepan. Over medium heat, shake the potatoes vigorously until all the moisture has evaporated and they are very dry. Beat in the butter. Beat together the egg yolks and the egg. Beat the mixture into the potatoes. Season with salt, pepper, and nutmeg. Beat until the mixture is smooth. Butter a baking sheet and spread the potatoes on it about 1-inch high. Brush them lightly with melted butter and chill in the refrigerator until very firm. Cut the potatoes into small oblongs and shape quickly into croquettes. Dip in egg white and bread crumbs. Fry in deep fat at 375°F. to 385°F. until golden on all sides. Drain on kitchen paper. Serve immediately.

Note: For skillet frying, make flat croquettes and brown them in shallow fat. These are good, but not as tasty as deep-fried croquettes. Croquettes can be kept warm in slow (300°F.) oven.

FLEMISH POTATOES

Pommes de Terre à la Flamande
Serves 4

One of the many excellent vegetable combinations found in Flemish cookery.

*1 large onion, thinly
   sliced
2 tablespoons lard or
   bacon fat
5 medium carrots, sliced
Salt and freshly ground
   pepper to taste*

*⅛ teaspoon ground
   nutmeg
⅓ cup water
5 medium potatoes, cut
   into 1-inch cubes
Beef bouillon or water
⅓ cup minced parsley*

Cook the onion in the hot lard until it is soft but not brown. Add the carrots and season with salt and pepper and the nutmeg. Add the water. Cook covered over low heat for about 5 minutes. Add the potatoes and enough beef bouillon to reach halfway up the vegetable mixture; the quantity depends on the size of the saucepan. Cook covered over low heat until the vegetables are tender. Check the cooking liquid; if there is too much, cook uncovered to let it evaporate, or if there is not enough to prevent scorching, add a little more bouillon. The finished dish should not be soupy. At serving time, stir the vegetables and sprinkle with the parsley. Serve with roasts or boiled meats or fowl.

Note: Exact proportions are not that important in this dish. The carrots and potatoes should be balanced with a few more potatoes than carrots. The main thing is to get the vegetables soft and not soupy, by adjusting the cooking liquid.

BOILED POTATOES

Pommes de Terre Nature

Boiled potatoes, with or without melted butter, and sprinkled with chopped parsley, are one of the standard accompaniments to Belgian fish and meat dishes when French-fries are not indicated. The potatoes are usually the main vegetable—that is, no other vegetable is served along with them, though a salad may appear.

Belgian potatoes are divine. First of all, there are half a dozen or so varieties which come at different times and serve different purposes. To eat them is sheer bliss. The potatoes for boiling must be floury (but not as floury as our Idahoes) and very dry, and, as a Belgian friend describes it, "sort of flakes have to be seen on the outside."

The potatoes, left whole, or cut in halves or quarters, depending on size, should be cooked in boiling salted water until they are barely tender. Drain the potatoes and return them to the saucepan. Over low heat, dry out the potatoes by shaking them so that they will not stick. Another way of making them mealy is to return the drained potatoes to the pot. Place a folded kitchen towel over the pot for 5 minutes. Shake the pot. Remove the towel, which will have absorbed any excess moisture. And if you want to be very sure that they will be perfectly dry, do as my mother did: serve the potatoes in a dish that has been lined with a folded table napkin. Arrange the napkin so that half of it overlaps and use the overlap to cover the potatoes to keep them hot and dry.

MASHED POTATOES, DUCHESSE POTATOES

Purée de Pommes de Terre, Pommes Duchesse

These potato dishes are just like ours, and the recipes can be found in any standard cookbook. What makes them Belgian, however, is the addition of a little nutmeg to their seasoning.

BRAISED POTATOES

Pommes de Terre au Lard

Serves 4 to 6

2 tablespoons lard	Water
3 slices bacon, minced	Salt and freshly ground
8 to 10 medium potatoes,	pepper to taste
peeled and quartered	⅓ cup minced parsley

Heat the lard in a heavy casserole and cook the bacon in it until it is soft but not brown. Add the potatoes and enough water to just barely cover the potatoes. Season with salt and pepper to taste. Cook covered for about 30 minutes or until the potatoes are tender. Shake the pan frequently to prevent scorching or stir carefully with a fork so as not to break the potatoes. Check for moisture; if necessary, add a little more water, a few tablespoons at a time, or if too liquid, cook uncovered until the excess liquid has evaporated. Sprinkle with parsley before serving with roast meats.

CREAMED SPINACH

Epinards à la Crème
Serves 2

Use 2 pounds of fresh spinach, and follow the directions for *Creamed Cabbage* (page 201).

Note: When washing the spinach, in several changes of water, remove the larger stems from the leaves, and shred the large leaves with a knife or with the hands. For most recipes, this does away with chopping the spinach when cooked.

SPINACH ROYALE

Epinards à la Royale
Serves 3 to 4

One pound of fresh spinach cooks to about 1 cup of spinach and 1 ten-ounce package of frozen spinach gives about the same. Spinach should not be cooked in an aluminum or iron saucepan because it easily picks up a metallic taste.

2 *pounds fresh spinach*
2 *tablespoons butter*
1 *tablespoon flour*
⅓ *to* ½ *cup milk or light cream*
2 *tablespoons grated Swiss cheese*

Salt and freshly ground pepper to taste
2 *eggs*
⅓ *cup heavy cream*
¼ *teaspoon ground nutmeg*

(*217*)

Preheat the oven to moderate (350°F.).

Wash the spinach in several changes of water. Remove any wilted leaves and tough stems. If the leaves are very large, tear them into pieces. Put the spinach into a glass, stainless steel, enamel, or earthenware pan. Bring to the boiling point. Lower the heat and cover the pan partly. Cook the spinach for about 5 minutes or until almost tender. Drain the spinach thoroughly and chop it fine or purée it in a blender. Heat the butter, stir in the flour, and cook, stirring constantly, for about 2 minutes. Stir in the milk and cook, stirring constantly, until the sauce is smooth and thickened. Remove from the heat, stir in the cheese, and season with salt and pepper to taste. Add the spinach to the sauce and blend thoroughly. Turn the spinach into a buttered 1-quart baking dish. Beat the eggs with the cream and the nutmeg. Pour the mixture over the spinach. Bake it for about 10 to 15 minutes or until the top is golden and bubbly. Serve immediately.

BRUSSELS SPROUTS

Choux de Bruxelles

These tiny firm buds, no larger than the nail of a finger, are a revelation to us Americans, accustomed as we are to the blowsy juvenile cabbages that, more often than not, pass as Brussels sprouts in our market. The only thing to do about this is to buy carefully in the first place, and in the second, to throw out all but the smallest sprouts.

Traditionally, they are cooked *à l'étuvée*—that is, gently steamed in a very little water with a nugget of butter, and seasoned, aside from salt and pepper, with nutmeg. The sprouts should be crisp and barely tender. I think this is the best way of eating all Brussels sprouts.

They should be cooked by themselves, since their flavor does not lend itself to combinations.

WINTER VEGETABLE CASSEROLE

Casserole Ardennaise
Serves 4 to 6

A good way of using up a ham bone. A vegetable casserole of this kind makes for a change from the usual vegetables. It goes well with cold cuts and roast meats.

*1 ham bone, trimmed of
excess fat and gristle*
6 medium carrots, sliced
4 small new turnips, diced
*2 leeks, white part only,
sliced*
*White, inner stalks of 1
bunch of celery, sliced*
*1 bunch green onions,
sliced*

1 garlic clove, minced
Boiling water
*4 medium potatoes, diced
(preferably new
potatoes)*
*Salt and freshly ground
pepper to taste*
¼ cup minced parsley

If the ham bone is very salty or a smoky one, cook it in boiling water for about 10 minutes and rinse it under running cold water to remove any excess flavor. Put the carrots, turnips, leeks, celery, green onions, and garlic in a casserole and place the ham bone on top of the vegetables. Add just enough boiling water to barely cover the vegetables. Simmer covered over low heat for about 30 minutes. Check occasionally for moisture; if necessary, add a little more boiling water. Add the potatoes and cook, covered and over low heat, for 15 minutes more or until the potatoes are tender. The cooking liquid should have been absorbed by then. Remove the ham bone, check the seasoning, and add salt and pepper if needed. Sprinkle with the parsley and serve very hot, from the casserole.

Note: This is one of the dishes where it is impossible to be accurate about the amount of water needed to cook the vegetables. This depends on the conditions of the vegetables themselves, on the shape of the casserole, on the heat, and so on. However, with a very little careful attention, this dish cannot go wrong.

XVI

---◄◆►---

---◄◆►---

Desserts and Cakes

---◄◆►---

CHERRY COMPOTE FROM THE ARDENNES

Compôte des Ardennes
Serves 6

2 *pounds dark sweet cherries, stemmed and pitted*

¼ *to* ½ *cup sugar, depending on the sweetness of the cherries*

½ *cup red currant jelly*

1 *cup dry red wine, preferably a full-bodied wine*

¼ *teaspoon ground cinnamon*

Peel of 1 lemon, yellow part only

Put all the ingredients in a deep saucepan. Bring to the boiling point and stir. Cover the saucepan and turn off the heat. Let the cherries stand for 10 minutes. Turn the fruit into a deep serving dish. Chill thoroughly, preferably overnight. Remove the lemon peel before serving and serve with macaroons or almond cookies.

Note: This excellent dessert is even better when made with the sweet-sour dark red Morello cherries that can occasionally be found in Italian vegetable markets. But plain sour cherries won't do.

STRAWBERRIES WITH LEMON JUICE

Fraises au Jus de Citron

Serves 3 to 4

It is surprising how few Americans know of the excellence of strawberries dressed with lemon juice and, if so desired, a little Kirsch.

1 quart strawberries
Sugar to taste
Juice of 2 lemons

2 to 3 tablespoons Kirsch
(optional)

Wash and hull the strawberries and put them into a serving dish. Add the sugar and sprinkle with the lemon juice and the Kirsch. Toss the berries to blend. Marinate for 1 to 2 hours and serve chilled.

STRAWBERRIES WITH WHIPPED CREAM

Fraises Chantilly

Serves 3 to 4

3 cups ripe strawberries,
hulled
½ cup superfine sugar
3 tablespoons tawny port
3 tablespoons Curaçao

3 tablespoons cognac
¾ cup heavy cream,
whipped, flavored with
1 tablespoon Curaçao

Put the strawberries into a crystal, china, or silver bowl. Sprinkle the sugar over the berries, and using a fork, mix carefully. Combine the port, the Curaçao, and the cognac and pour the spirits over the berries. Chill for at least 2 hours. At serving time, spread the whipped cream on top of the berries.

BAKED PEARS

Poires au Four

Serves 4 to 6

6 *large, firm Seckel or*   ¼ *cup butter, at room*
  Bosc pears   *temperature*
                          Vanilla sugar

Preheat the oven to slow, 300°F.

Wash and dry the pears. Rub them all over with butter and place them on a baking dish. Bake in a pre-heated oven for about 40 minutes or until soft. Sprinkle with vanilla sugar. Serve warm or cold, with plain heavy cream or a custard sauce.

For Vanilla Sugar: Cut 2 vanilla beans into halves lengthwise. Combine them with 1 pound sifted confectioners' sugar in an airtight container. Cover and let stand for at least 3 days. The sugar will smell and taste delightfully of vanilla.

UNCOOKED BLUEBERRY COMPOTE

Myrtilles à l'Encre

Serves 4

1 *quart blueberries*   *Dry red wine*
Sugar to taste

Clean and wash the blueberries. Put them into a bowl and add sugar to taste. Add enough wine to barely cover the fruit. Chill in the refrigerator for at least 1 hour, and serve with crisp sugar cookies.

AN UNCOOKED FRUIT CREAM

La Crème du Docteur
Serves 3 to 4

An easy, refreshing, harmless, and quick dessert.

1 large orange
1 large apple
1 cup chopped, drained
pineapple

¼ cup heavy or light
cream
1 tablespoon sugar

Peel the orange, removing the white inner peel. Cut into pieces, removing the seeds. Peel, core, and chop the apple. Combine the orange, the apple, the pineapple, the cream, and the sugar in a blender. Blend until the mixture is smooth, and chill before serving.

Note: This dish may be pepped up with any liqueur, rum, or Kirsch.

BETTY BOULPAEP'S FLEMISH RICE PUDDING

Rijstpap
Serves 4 to 6

This dish is as dear to the Flemish as apple pie to the Americans. It is different from the usual rice pudding inasmuch as it is flavored and colored with saffron, a spice highly regarded in Flanders, and shown off with pride. I quote Mrs. Boulpaep: "The Rijstpap *has* to be poured into a large and *flat* dish because then a large surface will show the golden color of the rice, and since saffron is very expensive, it is *important to show how yellow it made the Rijstpap.*" It is amazing how the saffron improves what is basically a bland dish, and I highly recommend this version to rice-pudding lovers. The Flemish sprinkle brown sugar over it.

1 cup Carolina long-grain	*1 ¼ teaspoon saffron*
rice	*½ cup sugar*
5 cups milk	*1 cup dark brown sugar*

Combine the rice, the milk, and the saffron in a heavy saucepan. Bring the mixture to a boil and reduce the heat. Simmer covered, stirring frequently, for about 25 minutes or until the rice absorbs the milk and the mixture is thickening. Add the sugar and cook, stirring constantly, until the sugar has dissolved. Pour the rice pudding into large, flat individual plates (see above) and cool. Serve the brown sugar separately at the table so that each diner may help himself.

SWEET-SOUR PLUM RELISH

Les Quetches au Vinaigre

About 2 quarts

A Walloon specialty, excellent with any kind of roast meat or fowl or cold cuts.

3 pounds purple Italian	*15 whole cloves, tied in a*
plums, ripe but firm	*little cheesecloth bag,*
1 ½ cups dry red wine	*together with 1 4-inch*
1 ½ cups red wine vinegar	*stick cinnamon*
2 ⅓ cups sugar	

Wash the plums. Prick each plum several times with a needle. Put the plums into a deep bowl, but do *not* use aluminum. Combine the wine, vinegar, sugar, and spices in a saucepan and bring them to the boiling point. Simmer covered over low heat for 10 minutes. Cool the mixture and pour it over the plums. Let the plums stand overnight at room temperature. The next day, drain the syrup from the fruit. Bring it again to the boiling point. Let it cool and pour it over the fruit. Let stand again overnight. The third day, transfer the plums and their syrup to a heavy saucepan. Cook over lowest possible heat until the plums' skins begin to tear in one or two places. Remove from the heat. Take out the plums with a slotted spoon and put them into sterilized jars. Boil the remaining syrup until it is the consistency of heavy cream. Strain it through a sieve and cool. Pour the cold syrup over the plums to cover them. Seal the jars in the usual manner.

RAISIN BREAD

La Cramique or Rosÿnenbrood
Two 9⅝ x 5½ x 2¾-inch loaves

This is Belgium's most popular coffee bread, and there are a number of variations, as with all basic recipes. This one makes a loaf that keeps fresh well, and has plenty of raisins. Betty Boulpaep, who developed it for me, told me that the Belgians say, when there are not enough raisins in *La Cramique*, that you need a bicycle to ride from one to the other.

This recipe calls for fresh yeast, which can be obtained at small bakery shops and also in supermarkets, in 1-ounce packages. I have not made it any other way, but the Fleischmann people, who make granulated yeast, tell me that 3 packages of granulated yeast correspond to 2 ounces compressed yeast, so that I imagine that a substitution would work out.

1 15-ounce package   *1½ teaspoons salt*
  raisins   *2 eggs, beaten*
2 ounces fresh yeast   *½ cup butter, melted and*
2 tablespoons sugar   *cooled*
2 cups lukewarm milk   *2 eggs, beaten (optional)*
8 cups sifted flour

Cover the raisins with lukewarm water and let stand for 1 hour. Drain and dry thoroughly between kitchen paper. Sprinkle the yeast and the sugar into the milk and stir until they are dissolved. Mix the raisins with the flour and the salt. Put the mixture into a large bowl or on a baking board. Make a well in the middle. Pour in the yeast-sugar-milk mixture. Add the beaten eggs. Slowly work in the flour from the sides of the well, using a fork. When the mixture holds together, knead for about 10 to 15 minutes, or until the dough is smooth and very elastic. Cover the dough and let rise in a warm place for 1 hour. Punch the dough down to its original volume. Divide it into 2 parts. Butter two 9⅝ x 5½ x 2¾-inch loaf pans and put the dough into them. Cover and let rise in a warm place for 1 hour.

Preheat the oven to hot (400°F.). Paint the surface of the loaves with the beaten eggs or with water so that the loaves will be shiny. Bake for about 1 hour 10 minutes. When done, the loaves will have a hollow sound when tapped and the edges will have worked away from the sides of the pans. Turn out of the pans. Cool completely before serving *La Cramique* rather thickly sliced, with coffee.

WAFFLES

Gaufres
About 16 to 18 waffles

There are any number of different kinds of waffles in Belgium. The one that is most characteristic is a thick waffle, at least twice as thick as our native waffles, which is crusty on the outside and soft inside. Waffle irons of this Belgian kind do not exist in the United States. However, the following recipe has the taste of a Belgian waffle, though not the consistency since the waffles have to be baked on our native irons, by necessity.

2 cups water
*1 ounce fresh yeast or 1 ½
  envelopes granulated
  yeast*
4 cups sifted flour
4 eggs, separated
½ cup sugar
2 cups milk

*10 tablespoons (½ cup
  plus 2 tablespoons)
  butter, melted*
½ teaspoon salt
1 tablespoon salad oil
*1 teaspoon vanilla
  flavoring*

Heat ½ cup of the water to lukewarm. Dissolve the yeast in the water. Put the flour into a large bowl. Stir in the egg yolks, the sugar, and the yeast. Beat in the remaining water, the milk, the butter, salt, salad oil, and vanilla. Beat until the mixture is smooth. Beat the egg whites until they stand in stiff peaks. Fold them into the batter. Let the batter stand for 1 hour, stirring it 4 times. Bake the waffles in a waffle iron as usual. Serve with whipped cream, fruit, jam, or sugar.

BRUSSELS BEER WAFFLES

Gaufres Bruxelloises
About 14 to 16 waffles

3½ cups sifted flour
½ teaspoon salt
⅓ cup salad oil
3 cups light beer
2 eggs

2 tablespoons grated
lemon or orange rind
1 tablespoon fresh lemon
juice

Combine all the ingredients in a deep bowl. Beat until the batter is smooth. Let stand at room temperature for 1 hour, stirring occasionally. Bake as usual.

Note: The beer ensures crispness and leaves no flavor whatsoever.

CHOCOLATE CAKE

Gâteau au Chocolat
Serves 6 to 8

An excellent cake, very chocolaty but made with only 2 tablespoons butter.

8 squares (8 ounces)
  semi-sweet chocolate
½ cup milk
½ cup sugar
2 tablespoons butter at
  room temperature
4 egg yolks

1 teaspoon vanilla
  flavoring
½ cup sifted cornstarch
1 cup blanched slivered
  almonds, slightly toasted
6 egg whites

Preheat the oven to slow, 325°F.

Over low heat, melt together the chocolate and the

milk. Stir in the sugar, and stirring constantly, cook until the sugar has dissolved completely. Remove from the heat and stir in the butter. Beat in the egg yolks, one at a time, and beat well after each addition. Stir in the vanilla. Beat in the cornstarch gradually, taking care that there are no lumps. Stir in the almonds. Beat the egg whites until they stand in stiff peaks. Fold them gently into the batter. Butter and flour an 8-inch spring-form pan generously. Turn in the batter. Bang a few times sharply on the kitchen table to let any air bubbles escape. Bake for 50 to 55 minutes or until the cake tests clean and has shrunk from the sides of the pan. Do not overbake. Loosen the sides of the pan and cool the cake. Serve with slightly sweetened whipped cream on the side.

DESSERT CAKE NAMUR

Gâteau Namurois
Serves 6 to 8

This rather dry, butterless cake keeps well. It is good with stewed fruit or a custard, or cut into halves and filled with jam, whipped cream, or butter cream. It is easy to make.

4 eggs, separated
¾ cup sugar
⅓ cup ground almonds
1½ teaspoons vanilla flavoring or 1 tablespoon brandy or liqueur

½ cup sifted flour
⅓ cup sifted cornstarch
Jam
Whipped cream

Preheat the oven to moderate 350°F.

Beat the egg yolks with the sugar for 5 minutes or

until the mixture is very thick and light. This is best done with an electric beater; the longer the beating, the better the cake. Stir in the almonds and the flavoring. Sift together the flour and the cornstarch and beat the mixture into the egg batter gradually, beating well after each addition. Beat the egg whites until they are very stiff. Stir ¼ of the egg whites into the batter and gently fold in the rest. Turn the batter into a well-buttered and floured 9 x 9 x 2-inch cake pan. Bake for 45 to 55 minutes or until a skewer inserted in the middle of the cake comes out clean and the edges of the cake shrink away from the side of the pan. Cool in the pan for 10 minutes and turn the cake out onto a rack. Reverse the cake so that it will cool right side up. The top will be beige, with whitish spots. Serve as it is, or cut into halves and fill with a tart jam or whipped cream. This cake does not need any icing, but the top may be sprinkled with sifted confectioners' sugar or masked with whipped cream or the cake, cut into halves, may be filled and frosted with *Betty Boulpaep's Mocha Butter Cream* (page 235) and decorated with halves of toasted almonds and glacé cherries.

ALMOND BREAD FROM BRUSSELS

Pain d'Amandes Bruxellois
About 60 cookies

4½ cups sifted all-purpose flour
1 teaspoon baking powder
1 teaspoon ground cinnamon
2 cups blanched almonds, ground

1¼ cup firmly packed light brown sugar
⅔ cup brandy
⅓ cup milk
½ pound (2 sticks) butter, melted

Into a mixing bowl, sift together the flour, the baking powder, and the cinnamon. Add the almonds and the sugar and mix well. Stir in the brandy, the milk, and the butter. Mix the dough with your (clean) hands and work it until it is homogenous and feels like clay. Shape the dough into a roll. Wrap it in wax paper or plastic wrap and chill it overnight. Preheat the oven to moderate (375°F.). Slice the dough into ¼-inch thick cookies. Butter and flour one or several cooky sheets and place the cookies on the sheets, leaving 2 inches of space between each cooky. Bake for 10 minutes. Remove immediately from the cooky sheet and cool the cookies on wire racks.

Note: 2 cups blanched almonds, ground, are not at all the same thing as 2 cups ground almonds. For this recipe, measure the blanched almonds whole and then grind them in a nut mill or in the electric blender. Do not use a meat grinder because it makes the nuts (all nuts) oily and not right for baking.

MRS. STONEHAM'S SPECULAAS

Speculau
About 80 cookies

Speculaas are the national cooky of Flanders (a crisp one) and brothers to the spekulatius of the Netherlands and northern Germany. These crisp spice cookies, whose origins go back for many centuries, are given to the children on St. Nicholas' Day, December 6, a great feast day when the Saint comes to reward the good children and punish the bad ones. Speculaas were—and are—frequently baked in splendid, elaborately carved wooden molds representing St. Nicholas and other figures. These molds, now eagerly sought by museums and collectors, belong to the artistic inheritance of the nation. An outstanding collection of these molds, some over five feet tall, belongs to Mr. Peter De Maerel of New York.

As in all traditional recipes, speculaas show slight variations which depend on the temperament of their maker; the recipe below, a delicious one, comes from a charming Belgian lady married to an Englishman.

½ *cup butter at room temperature*	*1 to 2 teaspoons ground cinnamon*
1¼ cup dark brown sugar, firmly packed	*2 cups sifted all-purpose flour*
1 egg, beaten	*½ teaspoon baking powder*

Preheat the oven to moderate (350°F.).

Cream the butter until it is light. Gradually beat in the sugar, a little at a time, beating well after each addition. (This is best done with an electric beater or mixer.) Beat 3 minutes longer. Beat in the egg and the cinnamon. Sift together the flour and the baking powder and stir it gradually into the batter. Mix the dough thoroughly. Generously butter a 15 x 11-inch baking pan. Pat the dough evenly into the bottom, smoothing it with a spatula. Bake the speculaas for 10 to 15 minutes or until the edges are beginning to get darker than the rest of the dough. Turn off the oven. Remove the baking pan and cut the speculaas at once into squares, diamonds, or any desired shapes. Return the pan to the oven for 5 more minutes. Cool the cookies in the pan for 2 minutes to firm them before removing them. Cool completely on racks before storing them in an airtight tin. These cookies keep well, but they must be stored in totally airtight tins or they will become soft rather than stay crisp, as they should.

BETTY BOULPAEP'S SPECULAAS

About 100 cookies

This is an excellent, very thin and crisp cooky. It is made somewhat differently than most American cookies.

4 cups sifted all-purpose flour

1 tablespoon baking powder

2 tablespoons ground cinnamon

½ teaspoon ground mace or ¼ teaspoon ground nutmeg

3 cups dark brown sugar, firmly packed

1 egg, beaten

¾ cup butter, at room temperature, cut into small pieces

2 tablespoons cognac

Cream the butter and add the egg. In a bowl, sift together the flour, baking powder, cinnamon, and mace. Add the brown sugar and mix all the dry ingredients thoroughly with the hands, then combine with butter, egg and cognac. Shape into a ball and let it stand at room temperature for 12 hours or overnight to allow the dough to ripen.

Preheat the oven to moderate (375°F.). Knead the dough once more, and shape it into 5 or 6 short sausages, with a diameter of about 1½ inches. Cut the dough with a very sharp knife into very thin slices. Butter several cooky sheets very generously. Put the cookies on the sheets, leaving about 2 inches between cookies to allow for spreading. Bake for 10 to 15 minutes, or until the edges of the speculaas are beginning to get darker than the rest. Check after the first 5 minutes of baking and after that regularly because the cookies burn easily. When they are done, take them out of the oven and let them cool for 2 minutes on the baking sheets to firm them. Cool them completely on a rack.

Keep the speculaas in airtight, iron tins, says Betty Boulpaep, because they do not stand humidity.

BETTY BOULPAEP'S MOCHA BUTTER CREAM

Crème au Beurre
To fill and frost a 9-inch cake

1 cup sweet butter (2 sticks) at room temperature
1½ cups superfine sugar
4 egg yolks

3 tablespoons very strong coffee
½ teaspoon vanilla flavoring (optional)

An electric beater is best for this recipe, since the sugar and butter must be thoroughly assimilated, which is a rather fatiguing thing to do by hand. Beat the butter until it is very soft and light. Gradually beat in the sugar, 2 tablespoons at a time, beating well after each addition. Total beating time should be no less than 5 minutes. Beat in the egg yolks, one at a time, beating well after each addition. Beat in the coffee and the vanilla. Chill the mixture until it is firm but still easy to spread, and fill and frost the cake.

CRÈME FRAÎCHE

In Belgium, as in France, the cream used generally for cooking and for eating with fruit and other desserts is *crème fraîche* or *crème double*. This cream is considera-

bly thicker than our American heavy cream and therefore better suited for thickening sauces, for instance.
The reason for the difference is that *crème fraîche* is
allowed to mature and to ferment very slightly. It also
has a somewhat nutty flavor and it is utterly delicious. In
America, we cannot have the exact cream they have in
Belgium, but a very acceptable way to achieve an American *crème fraîche* is given below:

For each cup of heavy cream, use 1 measured teaspoon
of buttermilk. Heat the mixture in a saucepan until it is
lukewarm (about 85°F.). Pour it into a glass jar and
allow to stand at room temperature until the cream
thickens. The temperature should not be lower than
60°F. and not higher than 85°F. In hot weather, the
cream can thicken in as little as 6 hours, in cold weather
in as much as a day and a half. Tightly covered, *crème
fraîche* can be stored in the refrigerator for 1 week.

Index

Nika Hazelton

Born in Rome, Nika Hazelton spent her early years traveling to the capitals of Europe with her father, who was a diplomat. She studied under Harold Laski at the London School of Economics and wrote for the *New Statesman* before coming to the United States to join the staff of *Fortune*. She began writing cookbooks during World War II and has been a cookbook expert for several magazines, including *Ladies' Home Journal, House and Garden* and *National Review,* and for *The New York Times Book Review.* Mrs. Hazelton is the author of *Reminiscence and Ravioli, The Art of Cheese Cookery, The Continental Flavor, The Art of Danish Cooking, The Art of Scandinavian Cooking, Chocolate, The Best of Italian Cooking, The Swiss Cookbook, Stew, The Cooking of Germany* and *The Picnic Book.*